Robert Kerr, Malcolm McLachlan Harper

Maggie o' the Moss

And Other Poems

Robert Kerr, Malcolm McLachlan Harper

Maggie o' the Moss
And Other Poems

ISBN/EAN: 9783744717533

Printed in Europe, USA, Canada, Australia, Japan

Cover: Foto ©Thomas Meinert / pixelio.de

More available books at **www.hansebooks.com**

Maggie o' The Moss;

AND OTHER POEMS,

BY

ROBERT KERR,

REDCASTLE.

EDITED, WITH A MEMOIR,

BY

MALCOLM M'L. HARPER,

Author of " Rambles in Galloway," &c.

"A few of the daft ideas of ROBERT KERR, loosely thrashed into rhyme, and written here for the gratification of his own whim, and for the perusal of a friend or two of his own kind of material and calibre, in the year o' good 1838."   [AUTHOR'S MS. BOOK.]

DALBEATTIE:
THOMAS FRASER.
1891.

CONTENTS.

	PAGE.
Preface,	ix
Memoir,	xi
Maggie o' The Moss,	1
The Old Moss Oak,	27
My First Fee,	30
The Pedlar and His Pack,	32
The Widow's Ae Coo,	39
Song,	41
Song,	43
Address to a Dog,	45
Song,	53
Song.—The Lass that Lives beside the Mill,	55
Cupid's Conquest,	57
John Frost,	59
An Autumn Eve,	62
Nanny Bell,	72
Song,	78
Address to a Corn,	79
The Plough's Address to Robert M'Kinnell,	83
Song,	85
Written in Robert M'Kinnell's Pipe-Music Book,	87
Lines on hearing that some of the Members, &c.,	88
Verses on the Death of a Young Lady's Lap-Dog,	88
Terry's Epitaph,	90
Song,	91
Lines on a Brother Rhymer, &c.,	94
The Poet's Epitaph,	95

PREFACE.

THE Editor and Publisher have cordially to thank the numerous subscribers for the hearty and liberal support which they have accorded to their efforts to present to the public, a complete collection of the Poems and Songs of ROBERT KERR. At the time of the Poet's death, the editor of the *Dumfries Courier*, judging from the poetic merits of "My First Fee," and "The Widow's Ae Coo," expressed the opinion that ROBERT KERR "must have left other effusions behind, which, if given to the world, would at once embalm his memory, and confer a favour on the public." Attention having been thus drawn to the matter so long ago, it is rather surprising that up till now no attempt has been made to publish his works in a collected form. But since the publication of *The Bards of Galloway* in 1889, where some of his pieces appeared, which were very favourably noticed by the reviewers, the Publisher has often been pressed to take the matter in hand. The present publication was, therefore, undertaken through such solicitations and repeated assurances that the work would be very generally appreciated. For purposes of the present compilation, the whole of the Author's MSS. were placed at the disposal of the Editor, as well as a large number of MS. copies of poems belonging to friends of the Poet. Most of the poems here reproduced have been taken from the manuscript books in which the Poet had written them with his own hand. Some few pieces have been omitted, which, in our opinion, the Poet, though leaving them in the MS. volumes possessed by his relatives, never intended for publication.

The preparation of the work has been to the Editor a labour of love, and it is to be hoped that the volume will be welcomed, not only by the friends and acquaintances of the Poet, but by all lovers of the literature of the province.

The Editor and Publisher would specially mention their sense of indebtedness to Mr Robert Kerr M'Neilie, and Mr Alexander M'Neilie, Metropolitan and Birmingham Bank, London; and Mr James S. Kerr, The Grove, Castle-Douglas, nephews of the Poet, for their kindness in granting them the use of the Poet's manuscript volumes; and to Mr James M'Kimm, Hardgate, who provided valuable information as to the Poet's early life and habits. To many other friends who have co-operated with them towards the success of the work their thanks are also due.

May, 1891.

MEMOIR.

ROBERT KERR was born at Midtown of Spottes, in the parish of Urr, Kirkcudbrightshire, on the 2nd September, 1811. His father, after whom he was named, was a native of the parish of Dunscore, Dumfriesshire. The maiden name of his mother, who belonged to the parish of Kirkpatrick-Durham, was Janet Shennan. There were six of a family — four sons and two daughters, and Robert was the eldest. His parents were generally respected for their industry, intelligence, and moral worth. The mother, especially, is represented as a woman of more than ordinary endowments. From her the poet inherited that tenderness of feeling and kindly human sympathy with those in distress which, as marked features of his character, are revealed in many of his poems.

In the life of Robert Kerr there is little to relate in the way of incident, or episode, of any consequence. So far as can now be gathered, he has left behind no prose letters that would reveal his habits of mind, his tastes in literature, or powers in that kind of literary composition. The only glimpses of the cast of thought of the inner man are now to be got from his poems, and a short manuscript diary, entitled his " Bosom Book," which, in estimating his character and manner of viewing the realities of life around him, will be referred to in the course of this memoir. Nearly all the contemporaries of his youth have passed away, and those of his manhood, who still survive, can give few, if any, reminiscences of him, or anecdotes illustrative of his ways of life, worthy of being reproduced here. Some of these, however, though trivial, are amusing to listen to, and show him to have had, like most true poets, a "dash of humourous eccentricity" about him. As a youth he was singled out as "original" amongst his fellows, and by all who knew him he is remembered as, at all times, possessed of a sunny disposition and a kindly, genial, sympathetic, and emotional nature, fond of seeing his fellow-mortals enjoying the "sweets" of existence, and entering fully into the fun and frolic of the social life around him.

At the Parish School of Hardgate he was instructed in the ordinary branches of education, under Mr William Allan, a successful teacher in his day, and

"A man of ready wit and talent,"

to whom as a sympathetic soul, an unusual characteristic of the pedagogue, the Poet addressed some of his juvenile lucubrations. Robert Kerr may be said to have "lisped in numbers," for when quite a boy he became known in the Village of Haugh and neighbourhood as a writer of verses.

He left school at an early age to assist his father in farm work, and for some years was employed in the ordinary duties pertaining to such a calling.

From incidental notes in his manuscript books, he appears to have taken an "honest pride" in having been like the great immortal singer, Burns, —a rustic bard wooing the muses while following the plough. These notes also give an insight into the circumstances under which some of his poems and songs were written, *e.g.*, the tale of "Nanny Bell" was composed one day in the spring of 1831, while driving a horse and cart at Redcastle. The "First Fee" was sent to the *Dumfries Courier* in the year 1843. "The Widow's Ae Coo" was inserted in the same Journal in the spring of 1844; and "The Old Moss Oak" was written 18th May, 1847.

Though the nature of Robert Kerr's employment was somewhat arduous at certain seasons of the year, the improvement of his mind was not neglected. He was studiously inclined, and very fond of reading,—traditional tales, Scotch stories, and poetry, being greedily devoured. The works of Allan Ramsay, Hogg, and Burns, were his favourites, and we can well imagine how from these founts of inspiration the boy's poetic fancy would be stimulated, when, like Burns, he pored over them at the family circle in the long winter "fore-nichts;" or "while driving his cart or walking to labour, song by song, verse by verse, carefully noticing the true and tender, or sublime, from affectation or fustian."

About the year 1826 he left his native valley and proceeded to Colchester, to push his fortune as a Scotch trader. A poem written in his fifteenth year expresses his feelings on leaving the district for a time, as follows:—

> "Where winding Orr flows to the shore,
>   Bedecked on every side
> With native flowers that sweetly pour
>   Their fragrant scents a-wide.
> These, native streams and dearest frien's,
>   I leave them for a while,
> Yet full intent, when time is sent,
>   Again to see my Isle.
> Then fare-ye-well, my friends who dwell
>   Along the banks o' Orr;
> Thy native Bard may yet be heard
>   Should he ne'er see thee more."

From his diary we find our poet to have been possessed, with all his frolicsome ways, of a contemplative and reflective turn of mind, continually in his early life and start in business, looking in upon himself and resolving to follow the good, and honest, course in his dealings with the world. In it he is revealed as a man of many moods. Like others of the tuneful tribe, there was in his nature "a contradictory mixture not only of grave and gay, of lively and severe, but of strength and weakness, of wisdom and folly." At stated intervals, but especially with the recurrence of his birthdays, he appears to have taken desponding and "remorseful retrospects" of his conduct, and being aware that his bias leant to the wrong side, framed rules and regulations for the better guiding of himself in his daily walk in life, and in conducting his business so as to be successful.

On 25th May, 1835, "It being exactly nine years since first I left my paternal roof in search of 'fickle fortune,'" he thus moralises :—

> "Three times three years have passed this day
> Since first I left my father's cot,
> And these nine years have passed away
> Like some tale told then half forgot.
>
> Yet memory points out here and there
> Some lines more deep and darker trac'd
> Of joy and pleasure, grief and care,
> That ne'er through life will be effac'd.
>
> Some things are past, which I can pass
> With pleasure, when my thoughts review—
> The greater part, alas! alas!
> Amendment—Oh! what room for you.

> Oh! thou Almighty one who rules supreme,
>   Who made the earth and still supports creation,
> From every idle, giddy, waking dream,
>   Arouse me up to take in contemplation.
>
> My ways, my means, my life, my situation,
>   The way I've acted and the worth of time,
> What I am now and what might be my station,
>   Possessed of health, and just now in my prime."

With Robert Kerr, as with the most of frail humanity, his bitter regrets for the past, and most solemn resolves for amendment in the future, ended in his

> "Whyles erring and whyles grieving."

The "spirit was willing but the flesh was weak," and, after all, his good intentions often ended in failure. So, occasionally, like others he had to lament "There are no resolutions ever I made that I have truly adhered to," and sensible that the "passions wild and strong," which he had by nature, required to be constantly kept in subjection, and that trusting in his own strength was of no avail, he thus passionately appeals to Heaven to help and direct him in carrying out his resolutions:—

> "Away, vain thoughts, let meditation
>   Be the only course for me.
> Let me take in contemplation
>   What I am and yet might be.
> Wavering mortal—wretched being,
>   Dost thou see thy years revolve,
> Yet not alter,—now All seeing,
>   Help me in my firm resolve."

From his youth upwards, our Poet had shown in all his ways that sturdy independence, in thought and action, which characterised the Scottish peasantry of his day. He had always a hankering after attaining to a position that would place him above the dread of want, and was ready to eschew all the pleasures and comforts of life to secure in the end "the glorious privilege of being independent." His thoughts were continually running in this direction—the "owre word" of all the philosophising in his "Bosom Book" being—

> "Firm resolved now and for ever,
> Foolish, idle, vain thoughts hence,
> Independence now or never,
> Now or never I commence."

To realise these longings for independence was no doubt the moving principle that actuated him in deciding to try his fortune at "The Pack," as he called it. In his time, the Scotch trade in England often proved lucrative to those engaged in it. Many young Scotsmen from rural districts, leaving, like him, the "trams o' the plough," had so successfully prosecuted the business as to be able, in middle life, to retire with a competency sufficient to allow of their spending the evening of their days in comfort and ease amid the scenes of their youth. From his knowledge of the success which had attended the efforts of some of his acquaintances in the trade, he would doubtless be induced to make this start in life. But, however much our Poet may have desired to get on in the world by imitating their example, such an occupation was ill suited for one possessed of his poetic temperament and tender sensibilities. With a heart overflowing with human sympathy, he would shrink from the hard and prosaic, worldly, and oftentimes selfish ways which many of those engaged in such a trade practised in order to be successful. Such a manner of life would pall on his sensitive nature, and we can well understand how, as a commercial man, the author of the "Widow's Ae Coo" was a failure. Had he been so constituted that like "The Laird of Fellend," graphically pictured by him in a lengthy piece unsuited, as a whole, for insertion in this volume, as one

> "Who bargained, who battled, who galloped, and ran,
> Who toiled through the week, and on Sundays would plan
> How to add to his £ s D,"

he might have succeeded; but with such sentiments as those revealed in his poem of "The Pack" and "The Autumn Eve," bad debts, with neither the heart nor the inclination to adopt pressing measures for their recovery, were sure to accumulate in his ledger. In such circumstances, it therefore showed a wise forethought on his part to relinquish the business, as there is no doubt he thoroughly disliked it, and longed to leave it for his place of "honour and of joy" behind the plough. Disappointed in his calling, and becoming indifferent to commercial success, his heart yearned to return to his former homely and natural ways of life. With what feelings of delight would he quit the din and bustle, and tainted atmosphere, of the crowded city for the fresh breezes of the hills, the green meadows, the trickling burns, and quiet sequestered nooks of rural beauty of the Urr Valley, there again to engage in agricultural pursuits—carting the hay from the scented meadows, rising with the lark to the plough, and mingling in the festivities of the rustics, whose homely manners and generous, hospitable ways he so much enjoyed. There he was truly in his element, free to follow the bent of his genius, and to draw from Nature the scenes and incidents embodied in his poems, the most popular of which are the outcome of his own experience. In his poem of "An Autumn Eve," he thus makes the genius of "The Plough" rejoice at his return :—

> "With joy I saw thee, native swain,
> Return home to thy land again,
> I proudly saw thee till the plain,
>   When Spring had sway,
> And viewed thee cut the yellow grain
>   This Autumn day."

Round the scenes of his early life were entwined the fondest sympathies of his heart, and his philosophic manner of looking on "men and things," and his love of nature in all her "shows and forms" unfitted him, like his older contemporary, William Nicholson, the Galloway Bard, for appreciating aright the genius of money-making. Mammon worship, or "the hunt for reputation, influence, place, or power," had, as he advanced in life, no attractions for him. The rustic obscurity of the Urr valley, and the primitive natural ways and manners of its inhabitants, were more congenial to his tastes. He preferred these, and the giving expression in rhyme to his "daft ideas" as he termed them, to making money; and, after all, when "life's fitful fever" was over, who will say he was not the gainer? He had the gratification in his lifetime of seeing some of his poems and songs become popular in the district, and we find that even now there are several who can repeat from memory many of them, which shows that they had taken hold of the popular ear, and had the genuine stamp of Nature upon them.

He may not have made money like some of those who started in the race with him, and floated prosperously along the stream of fortuitous circumstances, to positions of affluence and ease. But, on the whole, he enjoyed life a great deal more, and while many, if not all, of them are now dead and altogether forgotten, the author of "My First Fee" still lives, pleasing reminiscences of his happy social ways still linger in many a heart, and nothing but good is now spoken of Robert Kerr, "The Ploughman Poet of Urr." Such is the power of poetic genius, in giving its mead of immortality to those of "the heaven-born gift," over that of the worldling whose only desire in life is to amass wealth, and make a display of earthly possessions, while in death he goes to oblivion without a genuine tear of sympathy or kindly remembrance. In too many instances the only "friendly" attention he gets in departing, being that of impecunious lawyers over his "money-bags," and the distracting croaking of vulturous relatives, in their haste to divide the spoil.

The desire to be remembered when one is gone, and "to retain a cherished place in the love or esteem of some survivors," after the remains have been laid out of sight in the grave, is universal to mankind in this fleeting and transitory sphere. To the Poet, with his ardent aspirations for posthumous fame, it is the all and in all of existence. "To him there is the dearer life after life, and posterity's single laurel leaf is valued more than a multitude of contemporary bays." And it is natural to suppose that to Robert Kerr, with his poetic temperament, such thoughts would often recur, and that he would have some longings after the posthumous renown so dear to the heart of the Poet. Several of his writings give the impression that he harboured the thought that some of his poems would go down to posterity, and that in after years his name would not be forgotten. The following verse from his "Autumn Eve" reveals this :—

> "Continue still to weave thy lay,
> When at the plough, from day to day;
> Till o'er some fields where now you stray,
> And oft hast felt—
> The plough-boys yet unborn may say
> 'Here Kerr once dwelt.'"

Robert Kerr was only a few years in business in England. Nearly all his life he resided at Redcastle, engaged in work about the farm. He was a general favourite in the district, participating in, and enjoying the natural and simple ways of life in which his lot had been cast. In his day the habits of the people were more social and friendly than nowadays, when artificialism has to a great extent taken the place of nature in our domestic arrangements; and to the "hydra-headed" monster *Fashion* every one must conform, or merit the bann of *Society*.

The life amid which Robert Kerr spent his days was entirely free from the restraints and wearisome routine of the ways of modern society. Then there was a "greater individuality in thought and manner," and the drill of "adjutant Fashion" was not so much respected as it is now. To such a state of existence our Poet, with his vagrant ways, could never have conformed. The aphorism, "The poet is born and not made," is to a certain extent true, but circumstances of birth and surroundings have a great deal to do with the growth and development of the gift, and certainly the customs and natural ways of life in our Poet's day were more favourable to the growth of poetic feeling than that which we now lead. The harvest home, with its joyous festivities, and Halloween, with its train of curious superstitions, were rigidly observed by the rural population, and entered into and enjoyed without any qualms as to whether they were adhering to the strict rules of martinet fashion, and the etiquette of a refined society, or not. Other old observances and curious ceremonies, "involving the manners and customs" of our ancestors still lingered in the isolated district around the Haugh-of-Urr, and gave occasion for merry-makings, which are not known in our day. Our Poet was fond of these rural festivities, and being an invited guest to them all, contributed by his song, recitation, and witty conversation to the hilarity and enjoyment of the company. From his plain, unassuming manner and natural gifts, he was respected and looked up to as one of "light and leading" in the commonplace life of the district, but from what we can judge of his character and leanings, he would have been the very last to *pose* as the upright or perfect man of his social circle. He was, as we have seen, at all times sensible of his own failings, and when he had occasion to mark and tell his neighbours' "fauts and folly," his sarcasms, though pungent and cutting to the quick when exposing vice and hypocrisy, always leant to mercy's side when treating of human frailties. The sublime texts of "Scotia's poet king," that "the best may gang a kennin' wrang," and "to step aside is human," were his standard in judging of erring humanity.

So far as we learn from those who well knew the man in all his phases, there was in his nature "an entire absence of cant, hypocrisy, and hollow pretence, not in word and act only, but in thought and instinct." He was no ascetic—he was fond of society, and being tolerant of the moods and ways of those not so highly endowed by nature as himself, his company was often courted by his fellows, and at all the entertainments for instruction or amusement given in the place his services were in request, and in these amusements of the village he often took a leading part.

In the year 1839,

> "That vera year we had the muckle wun,
> Which levelled trees and hooses to the grun,"

Allan Ramsay's fine pastoral of the "Gentle Shepherd," being then the favourite play in the country, was acted by a company of local amateurs in the village of Haugh-of-Urr, for the benefit of the neighbouring poor. Our Poet composed and recited a prologue on the occasion, and—

> "Some country lads that doffed the sock and pleuch
> Donn'd sock an' buskin', an' did weel eneuch."

The "theatre" of the prologue being as usual the barn of the place, as we learn—

> "Doun Spottes burn street there was an auld laigh raw,
> And at the end o't leeved one John M'Wha—
> A decent chiel at this time kept a smiddie,
> Who gave his barn, and soon it was made ready."

We must now proceed to refer to his works, several of which are generally acknowledged to be the productions of a true poet, and are known far beyond the bounds of Galloway. Like Burns, whom he resembles in some respects, his poems and songs were composed and warbled with the lark behind the plough, or while tending his sheep on the hillside. He knew that to be natural in depicting the sentiments, the loves, and varied vicissitudes in the lives of those around him, he must go to Nature, and that—

> "The Muse nae poet ever fand her,
> Till by himsel' he learned to wander,
> Adoun some trottin' burn's meander,
> An' no think lang;
> O! sweet to stray and pensive ponder
> A heart-felt sang."

In his time predjudices and superstitious beliefs were prevalent in the district. Then the powers of warlocks and witches, now fallen into disrepute, were implicitly believed in by not a few. Ghosts, apparitions, wraiths, kelpies, and wirrikows, were so far credited, that even the most daring and sceptical considered it judicious on a dark night to keep, as Burns expresses it, "a strict look-out in suspicious places." Around the family circles the tedium of the winter "fore-nichts" was often beguiled by recounting and reading stories and traditions of the "on-goings" of these personages, which were so very ludicrous, that on the impressionable nature of the poet, they would have such an effect, as to be deeply engraven on his memory. The youthful and unfortunate poetic genius, Fergusson, pictures such a scene in his "Farmer's Ingle" in the lines:—

> "In rangles round, before the ingle's low,
> Frae gude-dame's mouth auld warld tales they hear
> O' warlocks, louping round the wirrikow:
> O' ghaists that win in glen and kirkyard drear,
> Whilk touzles a' their tap, and gars them shake wi' fear."

The subject of "Maggie o' the Moss," Robert Kerr's longest and most ambitious poem, was a real personage who dwelt in a cottage at no great distance from Redcastle. It was evolved from the following incident, related to us by one who knew the Poet well. "A reverend doctor, full of the joke, promised Maggie a pair of shoes if she would lift a man named M'Lelland, who was no bosom friend of the doctor's, and give him a long ride through the air. Maggie accepted the bribe, and carried out the stipulations, but landed too soon with her burden, in consequence of which the doctor only paid her with a pair of *clogs*. The man said he was lifted at his own door, and was carried at a rapid rate through the air—that he neither knew where or how far, but felt his feet brushing the 'tree taps' of a wood near his own house, and that he was set down at the precise spot from which he was spirited away." By the rural population of the district this tale was firmly believed, and poor Maggie, from her reputed evil eye and baneful spells, became an object of fear and dread to the dwellers in the neighbourhood. In this age of board schools, science, scepticism, and general enlightenment, the powers of witchcraft, the victims of which in past times in Scotland were often put to death under the most excruciating tortures, are generally scoffed at, and jeered out of court;

though even yet, in isolated districts far removed from railways, such superstitious beliefs have not altogether passed away.

When Robert Kerr wrote the poem of "Maggie o' the Moss," the subject, from being a popular one, would be read with interest. Now, it is mainly interesting as illustrating the manners and customs and superstitious beliefs of our forefathers, and as showing the author to have been possessed of imaginative and descriptive powers of a high order, with the happy gift of introducing, here and there, effective touches of light humour and satire. In the present day this piece, with some of his other productions, may be considered by many rather coarse in expression; but the reader in judging of this, must take into account the difference of the times and manners of the people fifty or sixty years ago. In giving expression to their natural sentiments and feelings, our forefathers were not so fastidious as we are now.

By his touching and pathetic lyric of "My First Fee," published in the *Dumfries Courier* in 1843, his name as a poet was first brought before the public. It has always been very popular in the district, and is now widely known. The genial editor of the *Dumfries Courier*, Mr John M'Diarmid, characterised it as an effusion "remarkable for its natural and graphic delineation of truth."

It was included in a recent publication, *The Bards of Galloway*, and was singled out by the reviewers of that work, as a piece containing touches of pathos that must appeal to every heart susceptible of human feeling. Mr W. S. Ross, a patriotic Gallovidian, himself a poet of great power and feeling, and possessed of high and varied literary attainments, noticed it in the *Agnostic Journal*, of which he is editor, in these very appreciative terms:—"This artless and touching idyl will compare favourably with anything of the kind in any language. It is a brief and simple entry in the annals of the poor, and, to those who understand the class of life it depicts, the very soul of pathos. With a wide knowledge of ballad lore, I can think of nothing at all comparable with 'My First Fee,' except Thom's 'Mitherless Bairn,' and Motherwell's 'Jeannie Morrison.'"

The poem was inserted in Hugh M'Donald's "Days at the Coast," as by an unknown author, and the Rev. P. Mearns, Coldstream, in his edition of Hyslop's Poems (1887) claimed it for that bard; but, so far as the evidence he was able to produce went, on entirely insufficient grounds. The writer of this memoir, as editor of *The Bards of Galloway*, in a note on Robert Kerr, which was considered to have fairly disposed of the question, reasserted the true authorship of the poem, and placed the laurel on the brow of the rightful owner, Robert Kerr. "The Widow's Ae Coo" and "The Old Moss Oak" have also obtained a wide popularity amongst the people. They are brimful of pathos and humour, and touch the heart as only true poetry can. Robert Kerr's place among the poets of Galloway will doubtless be variously estimated, but with these three poems he will always hold a respectable place among the sweet singers of the province.

In his later years our Poet had saved, or gained, the means which allowed him to take a farm of his own, and in the autumn of 1848 he removed from Redcastle to the farm of Bogue House, near Garliestown, Wigtownshire. He left Redcastle "full of health and hope, and with the fairest prospect of future usefulness," and a lengthened term of years before him. But the great Disposer of Events had ruled it otherwise, and the bright hopes of himself and friends were blasted. He had scarce settled down in his new home when he caught a cold, occasioned by a chill he had after bathing in the sea, which ultimately settled on his lungs, and ended in consumption.

After an absence of a few weeks he returned weak and emaciated to the paternal roof at Redcastle, and died there on the 30th September, 1848, "to the inexpressible grief of all who knew him," says a correspondent of the *Dumfries Courier* at the time, "including those who were nearest and dearest, not in the ties of kindred alone, but every warm emotion of the heart. The deceased was held in universal esteem by all within the range of his acquaintance. The kindness, frankness, and straightforwardness, of his disposition won their way to all hearts; and although no man was more modest, or as some would say, less presuming in the society of strangers, there was a nameless something in his manner, looks, and words that proved a passport to favour wherever he went. As might have been expected, his company was always welcome, a circumstance that increases regret the more that his death should have left a blank not easily supplied, adorned as his unobtrusive life had been by virtues that will be long remembered."

As a tribute to "departed worth and genius," the talented editor of the *Courier* republished " My First Fee;" and in an obituary notice feelingly remarked:—" The editor of this journal never saw the lamented deceased but once, and that only for a brief period. This was after the publication of " My First Fee;" and it was not his fault that no subsequent interview occurred, as Mr Kerr was pressingly invited to favour him with further opportunities of forming his acquaintance as often as he had occasion to visit Dumfries. The omission, he confesses, was his own loss, charmed as he had been with the first poem submitted to his notice, in common with many others, as was proved by its republication in distant and more influential journals."

Robert Kerr, until his last fatal illness, was a man of robust constitution. He was tall in stature, of a fair complexion, with an agreeable expression and intelligent piercing eye. The portrait prefixed to the volume, from a water-colour painting in the possession of his nephews, Messrs M'Neilie, late of Redcastle, being, we have been told, by those who knew the poet intimately, a very faithful likeness.

His remains lie in the family burying-ground in Urr Churchyard, a pleasant spot within sound of the gently rushing Urr, at no great distance from the place of his birth.

M. M'L. H.

CASTLE-DOUGLAS, May, 1891.

MAGGIE O' THE MOSS.

AMANG yon hills, where winding Orr
    Flows gently to the Solway shore;
Where moats and camps may still be seen;
Where trystes and tournaments ha'e been;
There stood a cottage, ca'd "The Bent,"
Where lived a couple weel content.
A cheerfu' body was the dame,
Wha never travell'd far frae hame;
Or fash'd wi' ither folk's affairs,
Or stories told of them or theirs;
But minded what was maist becomin'—
Her wark, like ony decent woman.
For pigs and poultry she could rear
As weel as ony ither near;
Could nurse her weans, and weave their hose,
Could mend their claes, and mak' their brose;
Wi' rock, few match'd her at the spinnin';—
As white as snaw she bleach'd her linen:
Could read her Bible, too, indeed—
Yea, had three-fourths o't in her head,

And said her prayers ilk' day did come—
They're seldom said, I fear, by some!
She never did attempt to claim
A richt to manage a' at hame;
But did her earthly lord obey,
As far's she thocht consistent lay;
Who was a man of honest fame,
And auld " Herd Simon " was his name.

His wife and weans were a' his riches;
His greatest dreid were ghaists and witches:
For in their power he put great faith,
And muckle did he dreid them baith!
But Simon's forte lay in his speaking
Where glasses rung, and punch was reeking;
For " mountain dew " could mak' him preach
Wi' sae much eloquence o' speech,
'Bout earth, and seas, and heavenly signs,
And knotty doctrines, and divines,—
That all who heard him were surpris'd
How he such learning realiz'd;
And swore he had been at some college,
And learn'd a deal o' wit and knowledge!

But, tho' he lik'd the " mountain dew,"
He ne'er, like some, got roaring fu';
'Twas little of it Simon bocht,—
Yet when he got a glass for nocht,—

Sim' aye ken'd what he was about,
He ne'er was ask'd to drink it out!
Nor was he very much to blame—
He got but little o't at hame:
He lik'd his wife, and ilka bairn,—
He gi'ed her a' that he could earn;
For she could lay that little out,
With great economy, no doubt:
Thus he did earn, and she did pay,
And I may venture here to say
A happier pair ne'er jogg'd through life
Than honest Simon and his wife.

   Scarce to the east, a good bow-shot
Off Simon's stood anither cot;
Where liv'd an ancient wither'd dame,
And auld "Witch Maggie" was her name,
For she by "Clootie" had been hir'd,
And sae that awfu' name acquir'd!
Her ghastly looks and visage queer
Were proofs to a' the nei'bours near:
Her crookèd back, and wrinkled brow,
Twa fiery e'en seem'd in a lowe,
Which had, perhaps—be't to their praise—
Bewitch'd some youth in former days:
Her curious muttering to hersel',
And where she cam' frae nane could tell;
Her odd-like manner, and her claes,

Made *a-la-mode* of former days;
A vulgar tongue, and rather free,
Made Meg what she was said to be!

    Ah! poverty, alas! alas!
    What ills attend thy humble class!
    How braid thy shouthers ocht to be,
    For ah! there's muckle laid on thee!
    Had Maggie been deck'd up wi' lace,
    For a' thae wrinkles on her face—
    Had she in warldly wealth been rich,
    Meg never had been termed a witch!
    But nae doubt Nick did constant wait,
    And tempted Maggie wi' the bait;
    He offered plenty every day,
    Sae Meg became an easy prey.
    Cauld-hearted want, my curse licht on ye!
    To spoil God's works the best and bonny,
    To drive an honest wife to error,
    Then live to be a country's terror!

  And here my story onward leads,
To tell o' mair o' Maggie's deeds;
For she was fear'd by poor and rich,
And noted far to be a witch;
Yet, in her calling nane abus'd her;
What e'er she ask'd for, nane refus'd her:
But every farmer strove to please

The hag, wi' milk, and meal, and cheese ;—
And nane considered it a loss
To serve auld " Maggie o' the Moss."

  Yet, aft wad Maggie play a trick,
To prove her colleague-ship wi' Nick;
For they, wha Meg's petitions spurn'd,
Had cairts, and carriages o'erturn'd ;
Their horse gaed mad, and ran like stags,
Till some got broken arms, and legs ;
The best kye in the byre gaed yell ;
Some died, some couldna raise themsel' :
In short—ilk' beast the farmer had
Died,—sicken'd,—rotted,—or, gaed mad !

  And aft had Maggie raised the wun',
And muckle mischief had she done ;
When storms blew loud at dead o' nicht,
High in the air she took her flicht :
Of raging storms, she led the van,
And like a shade swept o'er the lan' ;
Whyles skimming o'er some mountain's brow—
Leaving the valleys far below :
Whyles circling, like a bird o' prey—
Flying through ether far away ;
Now driving close o'er earth she scuds ;—
Next moment darting through the cluds,
Now shaking corn in certain spots,

Now tirling kirks, and country cots;
Now plunging in the depths of ocean,
And setting all in dire commotion;
Now sinking ships was her employment;—
The mae she drown'd the mair enjoyment!

  And aft had Meg, as nei'bours tell,
To shape of hare transformed hersel';
When in that form, had aft ta'en place
Mony a noble weel run chace:
Nae grey-hound e'er was Maggie's master;
Nae hound ran fast, but Meg ran faster:
Nae collie ever kept near till her;
Nae sportsman yet was fit to kill her:
For Maggie wad ha'e ran sae wanton
Thro' hedge and ditch, through field and plantin':
O'er hill, and dale, sae fast she'd scud,
Wi' flatten'd ears and cockèd fud;
That wi' Eclipse, the far-fam'd racer,
It would have been as vain to chase her,
As 'tis for mortals of this zone
To seek the philosophic stone!

  And aft, at nicht, ane black as soot,
Wha seem'd to wear a cloven foot,
Wad visit Meg's—for on the green,
Next morn, strange footsteps aft were seen;
And by her well, each gloomy nicht,

Will o' the wisp's deceitfu' licht,
Within a quagmire, to decoy
The traveller and the errand-boy :—
And her auld cot amang the trees,
Did mony a nicht seem in a bleeze ;
Frae midst of which was heard the noise
Of hellish revelry and joys—
But when the morning came serene,
Still stood her cot as nocht had been,
And muckle mair that provèd weel
Meg maun ha'e dealings wi' the De'il.

 Auld Simon, wha nane had offended,
But they wha only ill intended,
Wi' Maggie's tricks was weel acquainted,
And lang wi' Meg had been tormented.
Ae nicht had Maggie changed her form,
And, like an eagle in the storm,
Wi' hideous yells she filled the air,
And tirled Simon's cottage bare ;
And by some cantrip spell o' Meg's,
His ducks had a' laid wounded eggs ;
His tappin'd hen, a favourite burdie,
By Maggie's craft, had ta'en the sturdy,
Which did poor Simon sae provoke,
He swore he would stand nae sic joke ;
But on himsel' took solemn vow
That he some day would score her brow ;

And rid himsel' o' a' thae evils
In spite o' Meg and a' the deevils
That ever wrocht an incantation
In this, or ony ither nation!

 Ah! Simon! sair ye did repent
Your hasty vow and rash intent,
Ye little kent what Meg wad play
Wi' you for that some ither day;
Ye little thocht ye had to flee,
Far, distant far, beyond the sea;
Thro' chaos' bounds to meet auld Cloot,
Whilst Maggie rode thee like a brute;
Which chanc'd ae nicht to be thy fate,
As I mean shortly to relate.
My rustic muse, ye maunna fail,
Whilst I recite the awfu' tale:
And such a tale,—the Lord look o'er me!
As never mortal mou'd before me.

'Twas when dark winter rul'd the time,
And Sol beam'd faintly on our clime;
The day had fled, and o'er the nicht
The moon-beams shed their silver licht;
The twinkling stars look'd frae the skies
Wi' smaller, but wi' sharper eyes;
The settled air was calm and still,
And far resounded every rill;

The loud hoarse bark from scatter'd domes
Proclaim'd who watch'd the farmer's homes;
The whistling wild fowl left the lakes,
To seek unfrozen springs and brakes;
For biting frost had bound the soil,
And kept the ploughman frae his toil;
The curlers now had left their play,
Expecting more the coming day;
For still the atmosphere felt keen,
And clouds were nae where to be seen,
But all round, an unbroken view
Of orbs of light, 'midst realms of blue,
Plac'd in the heavens to move or stand,
By Order's great unerring hand.

Auld Sim', wha did but seldom roam,
Did chance that night to be from home;
His road was langer than the day
Sae night o'ertook him in his way,
Yet still he thocht himsel' secure
Frae witch, or de'il, or evil-doer;
The road was short he had to gang,
But there were fleysome pairts amang;
Wi' lengthen'd stride he on did jog,
Whyles o'er a knowe, whyles in a bog;
Whyles round some mire he took a turn,
Whyles stepping o'er some wimpling burn;
Whyles speiling dykes, and louping ditches,

Richt gled he had got free frae witches!
Still stepping on, he reach'd the heicht,
And gladly saw his cottage-licht;
When all at once, to his surprise,
A figure stalk'd before his eyes.
Approaching near, it stood before him,
Whilst an increasing dread came o'er him!
Auld Meg's phys'og he weel did ken,
Ilk' bristled hair stood up on en';
Aff flew his bonnet and his wig,
Each limb shook like an aspen twig;
His heart deep dreading something ill,
Went like the clappers o' a mill.

Thus Simon stood, like ane rebuk'd,
And naething said, but fearfu' look'd,—
Nor had he power to say "guid e'en,"
Or, "pray, dear nei'bour, where ha'e been?"
Nor for his life could lift a leg,
To try to save himsel' frae Meg;
But like Lot's wife, in ancient time,
Was turned a pillar for her crime;
So Simon stood, a statue carnal;
Whilst Meg rag'd like some fiend infernal;

Now like a wild beast mad for prey,
It's hungry cravings to allay;
Like baudrons when she sees a mouse,

Or falcon when he sees the grouse;
Like ocean's monsters in their flicht,
That dart at what's before their sicht;
Sae Maggie flew wi' furious haste,
And made poor Sim' the cauld earth taste;
Then cross his haunches striding o'er,
She gave him the command to soar:
At first poor Simon, sweir to yield,
Held hard and fast the frosty field;
His body now earth's surface spurn'd:
He seem'd like gravitation turn'd;
His heels went bickering in the air,
He held till he could haud nae mair:
Till first wi' ae han', syne the tither,
He lost his haud o't a'thegither;
And mounted up in gallant style,
Right perpendicular for a mile.

 Ah Simon! when thou wert ascendin'
Why didst thou not touch every tendon?
Bow down thy head—kick up thy heel,
And twist and wallop like an eel?
And throw the carlin aff thy back,
Till on some craig her head play'd crack?
Or broke the charm, and when ye fell
Kept Meg beneath and saved yoursel'?
But that was far frae Simon's power,
He fand't impossible to throw'er;

For brawly ken'd she how to ride,
And stick richt close to Simon's hide;
For aft had Maggie on a cat
Across the German Ocean sat;
And wi' auld Nick and a' his kennel
Had aften crossed the British Channel;
And mony a nicht wi' them had gone
To Brussels, Paris, or Toulon;
And mony a stormy Hallow e'en,
Had Maggie danced on Calais green!

But Maggie had that nicht to gang
Through regions dreary, dark, and lang,
To hold her orgies in a place
Which men denominate, "unknown space:"
Where a' the witches were to gether
Between this world and the nether;
And there wi' Nick to hold levee,
Besides some glorious jubilee;
To celebrate some fate renown'd,
Such as, when Pharaoh's host was drowned;
The morn when our first parents fell;
Or Satan's self broke loose frae hell.
Yet such a nicht it chanced to be
As even witches seldom see;
For Satan's self had given orders,
Thro' ev'ry nook of the earth's borders,
That ilka warlock, witch, and elf,

That nicht half-way should meet himself;
And they unanimous did chuse
The northern pole for rendezvous;
Where a' should meet their different legions,
Ere they flew to the dismal regions!

Now to the northern Simon flies,
Like smoke that floats 'tween earth and skies,
Or like November's misty rain,
That speedy drifts alongst the plain;
Wi' Maggie mounted on his back,
As sicker as a pedlar's pack:
Wi' raip about his head and neck,
Her human pony to direct;
And in the other wither'd hand
A hazel cudgel did command;
With which she play'd upon him sweetly,
And leather'd Simon's sides completely!

Not *sweet* for him, alas, poor Simon!
Fain wad he thocht he was but dreamin';—
Fain thocht his brain was in confusion,
And nothing but a wild delusion!
A man micht fancy, that he star'd,—
A man micht fancy, that he heard;
But there was one of no denying,
Which prov'd to Simon he was flying;
And tho' he knew not, where nor whence,

Convincing feeling—noblest sense,
In no ways could be disbelieved—
He felt too well to be deceived.

The night, which had been calm before,
Now chang'd, and winds began to roar:
The moon had set clean out o' sicht,
And dark and dismal grew the nicht;
And ay the louder blew the blast,
Our flying hero flew mair fast;
And furious rush'd, wi' whizzing din,
Against the frosty northern win',
Which round that head devoted, blows,
Enough to split his very nose!

And thus 'tween heaven and earth they swept,
Meg at no regular distance kept;
But whyles ascended, till our Planet
Seem'd to the sicht as wee's a wa'nit;
Then sinking lower by degrees,
She rubs his nose against the trees;
Or dips his wame in some moss hole,
Wi' nose still pointed to the pole!

Like swallows near the gloaming licht,
As o'er a lake they tak' their flicht;
How swift they skim the liquid plain,
Then mount up high in air again!

Now down themselves again they fling,
And skiff the water on the wing;
So, o'er our Isle, and far ayont it,
Poor Simon flew, wi' Maggie mounted!
For as the precious hours o' nicht
Flew by, sae Meg increas'd her flicht;
And o'er the frozen ocean vast,
The domicile of many a blast,
She darts away o'er frozen sails,
O'er shaggy bears, and spouting whales.
Here icy mountains huge are seen,
There struggling ships were jamm'd between,
And onward still she takes the rout
O'er seas no British charts laid out,
And skims the icy rattling tide,
Wi' icicles on every side:
Her nose and chin, her auld gown tail
Were cased in ice like coat o' mail.
A magnet made by magic art,
Gat frae the de'il in some black part,
Made Meg acquainted wi' the sphere,
And tauld the pole was drawing near,
Till by the streamer's flitting licht,
Which glented brichtly through the nicht,
She spied at length the very part,
And like a bird wi' cheerful heart
Alighted gently on a knoll,
Beside the much-sought arctic pole.

What pencil could the picture draw!
What tongue could tell what Simon saw!
What multitudes were gather'd here
Frae every airt the wind can steer:
Here mounted upon bears in raws,
Appear'd the hardy Esquimaux;
Here Indian carlins on bamboos,
And south sea hags on kangaroos;
Here sturdy witches of the arctic,
Kiss'd warlocks frae the far antartic;
And mony a Caledonian grannie,
Flown aff wi' some auld nei'bour Sawnie;
Some rode on ragworts, some on docks,
Some lang kail runts and cabbage stocks:
Some on a cat, some on a hen,
And some upon their ain guidmen;
For tho' the power lay wi' themsel's,
To ride wi' nocht wad break their spells.
So some had ponies wanting saddles,
Some cuddies—some on wooden ladles.
What shouts and yells rose wildly there!
A thousand lingoes rent the air!
When rising like a swarm of bees,
Or craws when hame-bound to their trees,
At once the solid earth they leave,
To meet the fiend wha ruined Eve.
Soon out o' sicht o' earth they fly,
And now they canna see the sky,

Quick flying—straining—sweating—frothing,
They stretch, they strive, 'twas neck or nothing;
For wha got first they ken'd fu' weel,
Wad get some present frae the De'il.

But now to tell of things below,
A while my muse must let them go,
Pursuing on their destinations,
Wi' nae zig-zag oscillations,
But onward furious fast they fly,
As Time's wings to Eternity.

By this time Nick, the great arch-fien',
In hell a meeting did convene;
And mounting on a brumstane rock,
Thus to the other fiends he spoke;
And tho' got rather hoarse wi' reek,
His farthest subjects heard him speak,
And listen'd with a due respect,
His words which were to this effect:

" Doom'd sons below, the time draws near,
When your arch-brother must appear,
Far in the empty realms o' space
To meet there at a certain place,
That race of which our share we claim,
Sprung from that planet—Earth by name.
Noo Bluefire, ane o' my best de'ils,

This moment you must ply your heels,
Put on your best and swiftest wing,
Fly up to earth, and you must bring
Twa kegs o' best Jamaica rum—
We'll meet you half road as you come,
With which I'll treat, as sure's I'm curst,
The clever jade that meets me first!"
So rising up away he started,
Still leaving charges as he parted,
And soon came to (upon his pinions)
The John O' Groat's o' his dominions:
The porters knew their maister weel,
The gates were op'd—out flew the de'il—
Charg'd them to warn him of disorders,
Then at a dart he clear'd the borders,
And far in emptiness set sail,
With a long ret'nue at his tail.

 Ah Nick! I doubt—yea, maist can tell,
Ye dinna rule your family well!
For had it been but rightly headed,
Ye surely never wad hae dreaded
A wild rebellion rise within it,
In your being absent for a minute!

 Alas! man should take thy example,
And strive on fellow man to trample—
'Tis plain in your abode, and here,
A despot always rules in fear!

Far, far in space, and void of sky,
The ruins of some world gone by;
(Or what perhaps had been a sun,
But now for want o' fuel done),
Composed of lava, in and out,
Upon its centre, wheel'd about,
Wi' nothing living on its face,
Nor did it alter from the place;
But whirl'd in darkness evermore.
So to that spot did Satan soar,
And, carving out a cinder throne,
Sat down and waited for his own.

But to our witches,—on they flew,
And lo! what's this appears in view?
'Tis fire—'tis light—'tis coming fast,
It must be day—alas! 'tis past!
At first poor Simon's heart grew fain,
He thought it was the world again:
But human hopes are often vain,
And fancied pleasures turn to pain;
Nae world was here, nae licht o' day,
'Twas but a comet on its way;
Which gleam'd one moment on the core,
And left them darker than before;
Wi' nocht to licht them to the prize,
Except the gleam o' Satan's eyes:
Which now, at distance 'pear'd in sicht,

Like glow-worms in a gloomy nicht:
Making our witches fly like win',
Leaving the wizards far behin';
For warlocks tho' they wear the breeches,
Hae never ony chance wi' witches.

Wi' joyfu' heart Nick spied them comin',
And roar'd out—" O delightful woman!
Tho' whyles I've lost a point by thee,
You've been a charming friend to me:"
Then betted part o' his dominions
Upon the race and his opinions;
Whilst different members o' his clan,
Oft times wad bet him "three to wan."

Cries one, upon his bended knees,
" My liege, I'll bet you if you please,
That Bess o' Borgue will Meg defy."
" She may," quo' Nick, " but time will try."
" A murderer's head I'll bet she lose it."
" Psha! psha," cries Nick—" Meg wins the brose
    yet."
" What's yon she rides wi' stretchèd lim'?"
" What! pray sir, do ye no' ken him?
'Tis auld herd Simon o' the Bent,
Ane wha I think will ne'er repent;
For mony a wicked trick, you know,
He's in our ledger long ago."

Maggie o' The Moss.

"That's richt," quo' Nick, "I mind richt weel,
When teaching some young awkward de'il;—
I'm sure it must be half a cent'ry—
We had his name in double entry."

Whilst thus they betted, far ahead,
Four carlins seem'd to tak' the lead—
'Twas "Bess o' Borgue," and "Glencairn Kate,"
Wha baith on Broomsticks had their seat;
Our auld acquaintance made out three,
The fourth cam' frae the Southern sea,
A wrinkled hag o' visage copper,
And firm resolved nae ane should stop her;—
Weel mounted on a kangaroo,
And at a furious rate she flew:—
Strove sair—but couldna gain an inch,
Even Satan's sel' was at a pinch
To name the winner—loud he swore,
He ne'er saw sic anither four;
Till getting nearer to himsel',
In shorter time than tongue can tell,
They spring—they dart—now quick, then quicker,
'Twas now or never for the liquor.
Now Bessy seems to tak' the lead,
Now Maggie's first by half a head:
Now Katie's winning plain's can be,
Now Copper beats the other three;
The vera twinkling o' an eye

Behind, and Bessy will get by,—
One final effort—three must lose,
'Tis won by—" Maggie o' the Moss,"
Who bounding off her fainting steed,
Sprang forth to Nick wi' lightning speed,
Who clasping Meg in warm embrace,
Proclaim'd her winner o' the race.

Few minutes had got time to wear,
Till witch and wizard a' were there,
The loud harangue of welcome o'er,
For dancing they prepar'd a floor.
Nick gave the orders to his band,
And taking Maggie by the hand,
(His greatest fav'rite a' the nicht,
While ither pairs were plac'd a' richt)
Inquir'd what tune she pleas'd to ha'e,
" What tune ? " quo' Maggie—" ' Clean pea strae ; '
Or there's anither which I prize,
' Yersel' flown aff wi' the excise.' "
" Weel spoke my partner," cried the De'il,
" Nocht beats a gude Scotch dance or reel : "
Now rose the music soft and sweet,
Now Maggie starts, and what a treat!
As round she flies wi' Satan's sel',
Though whyles nigh trippèd by his tail ;
Whilst he beat nimbly wi' his cloots,
In spite of breeding and of boots,

Till mony a carlin envied Meg,
And wish'd to see her break her leg.

 The dance scarce o'er, Nick did begin
A solo on his violin,
And sweetly play'd upon ae string,
While Maggie danc'd the "Highland Fling;"
He play'd his shifts wi' sic an airt,
And Meg sae supple did her pairt,
As would ha'e sham'd, if shame therein is,
Your German and Italian "ninis."

 By this time Blue-fire had arriv'd,
And doon amidst the black throng div'd—
Brocht forth the kegs without delay,
Presenting Maggie wi' the twae:
He'd snatch'd them off a smuggler's nag,
And brain'd its driver o'er a crag;
Which did his master sae delicht,
He made him on that instant knicht,
Wi' star and ribbon "quite a swell,"
The "order" Simon couldna tell;
For 'twas enough, from what he saw,
To fright sense, memory, and a'.
Yet Simon recollected well,
And mony a lang year liv'd to tell
What reels they danc'd, and how they play'd
Strange antic tricks in masquerade;

And how the gloomy caverns rang,
Re-echoing the witch's sang.
And how before they would retire,
Of earth's affairs Nick did inquire,
Which they as willing did unfold,
And many a horrid tale they told
Of many a dark device and plan,
The cruel tricks of man to man ;
Of stretchèd necks and broken banes ;
Of poison'd wives and smother'd weans ;
Of widows where there should been nane ;
Of orphans cheated o' their ain ;
Of deeds did I but tell a part,
The blood would curdle round my heart.

Loud laugh'd auld Nick, and danc'd and reel'd,
And cleverly his pains conceal'd ;
For could his black heart been laid bare,
Wretch'd fiend, nae frolic lodgèd there.

   Ah ! Satan is it thus with thee ?
Above, below, thou'rt never free.
Could leagues unnumbered frae thy den
Not in the least appease thy pain ?
Could dancing witches, which did please thee,
Not in the least iota ease thee ?
Ah ! no, though distant frae thy hame,
Thou art a demon still the same:

> Locality's a small affair,
> When hell is with thee everywhere.

Prepar'd at last to take their flicht,
Yet loath to bid his friends good nicht,
Nick bade his menials go and look,
If Simon still was in their book.
Down dropt our hero as if shot,
His cares and fears were a' forgot;
His nostrils seem'd devoid of breath,
And every muscle cauld as death,
Yet life was there, and death would win' him,
His soul was scarcely out or in him;
Hard struggled death and life for sway,
Till life victorious won the day,
His senses gether'd by degrees,
He first felt life, tho' not at ease;
His ears neist caught the roaring main,
And recollection came again,
When bold at length to ope' his eyes,
What joys, what transports, what surprise!
He spied, which made his pulse to play,
The dark blue hills o' Galloway;
And by his sides the twa prize kegs,
Strapp'd o'er his back wi' Maggie's legs;
Who sat atween the twa erected,
Smoking her cutty quite collected,
Flying alongst the way they came,
Within a mile or twa o' hame.

Our hero and our heroine
Had now reach'd where they left yestreen;
When some kind cock, to morning true,
As if by more than instinct crew:
Loud screigh'd auld Meg, the cantrip spell
Was broke, and down baith birling fell;
But by good luck the kegs o' rum
Did happily beneath him come,
Or in a moss-hole out o' sicht,
Poor Sim' had finishèd his flicht;
And never lived to tell what past,
A tale o' wonders that may last,
Whilst witches dwell upon the earth,
Whilst Orr flows to the Solway Firth,
Till death's wark's done, and Nick has got him,
And time's lang sinks lie at the bottom.

   Yet should some future sceptic sinner,
As fond of doubting as his dinner,
To show the clearness o' his brain,
Strive to confute our story—when
The village Blacksmith and the Bard,
And parish Sexton's nae mair heard;
When Jamie nae mair tolls the bell,
And Johnnie's hammers cease to knell;
When Robin quits his plough and toil,
And rests his banes beneath the soil;
When mony a wife that could declare

The truth is gane guid kens na where.
'Tis then, perhaps, some rising twig,
Wi' bumps of learning unco big,
May prove,—prove what? why prove no more
Than what has oft' been shown before;
That Maggie doesna rank alone,
Nor yet is Nick the only one
Who oft' has guiltless caught the blame,
By having first a wicked name.

LINES ON DIGGING UP AN OLD MOSS OAK.

 HAVE raised thee again to the light, Old Oak,
  And thy huge dark trunk appears
From the bed where thy age, or the light'ning's stroke,
  Had laid thee some thousand years.
Was't the wind, or the wave, that thou couldst not brave,
  Or when or how didst thou fall?
I have much, old tree, to inquire of thee,
  And would thou couldst answer me all.

Didst thou flourish in a distant time unknown,
    Ere man walked the world erect,
When the giant Mammoth and Mastodon
    Would range through the forest uncheck'd?
Or did'st thou spread thy broad crowned head
    In days when the human race,
In their pomp and pride, stretch'd far and wide
    O'er earth's gay flow'ry face?

Then gallants, vigorous, stout, and bold,
    Who seven score years had seen,
Did they dance with the girls, a hundred years old,
    Beneath thy bows when green?
And the man who had seen eight centuries pass,
    Whose eyes were turning dim,
Did he rest in thy shadow? Alas! alas!
    I should liked to have talked with him.

Wert thou a tree when the waters arose,
    And deluged our world below?
Were the nestlings drowned on thy topmost boughs
    Four thousand years ago?
The parents that on weary wing filled the air,
    And the men that long did scoff,
Did they clutch at thy twigs in their dark despair,
    While the wild waves dashed them off?

Or did'st thou bend o'er a barbarous race
    In a much later date and day,
Who sought thy shade as the worthiest place
    To kneel to their gods, and pray?
Has the altar rude by thy old trunk stood
    Where men would in vain implore?
Has the victim bled, and thy roots been fed
    With the dark rich human gore?

But in vain, old tree, do I ask of thee,
    Thou hast long, long lain unknown:
Thou hast flourished somewhere, thou hast once been fair,
    But thy date and thy history's gone;
And such is our lot, soon unseen—forgot
    When my bones may be cast on the green,
It is but like a day till the living will say—
    "Ah! look here where some dead man's been."

MY FIRST FEE.

Y mither was wae, for my faither was deid,
    An' they'd threaten'd to tak' the auld hoose owre oor heid;
Her earnin's grew scanty, the meal was got dear,
An', the auldest o' five, I could whyles see the tear,
When she cam' hame at nicht, glisten bricht in her een,
Half hid, as if't didna juist want to be seen;
I spoke na a word, but my wee heart wad ache,
An' I wished I was big, for my puir mither's sake.

There were fermers aroun' wanted herds for their kye,
And my mither had said she had ane that wad try;
I mind hoo I trembl'd, half fear, an' half joy,
When a maister ca'd on us to look at the boy:
He bade me stan' up, an' he thocht I was wee,
But my frank, honest face, he said, pleasèd his e'e;
He wad tak' me, and try me ae half-year, an' see,
For a pair o' new shoon, an' a five shillin' fee.

We were gled to hear tell o't, the bargain was struck,
An' he gied me a saxpence o' earles for luck;
My trousers an' jacket were patch'd for the day,
An' my mither convoyed me a lang mile away,

Wi' charges an' warnin's 'gainst a' kin' o' crime,
An' rules she laid doun, I thocht hard at the time:
If the kye should get wrang, I was never to lee,
Though they sent me awa' but my shoon or my fee.

Sae I fell to my wark, an' I pleas'd unco weel—
But a word or a wave, an' I plied han' or heel;
But my troubles cam' on, for the fences were bad,
An' the midsummer flees made the cattle rin mad;
An' in cauld blashy weather, sair drenched wi' the rain,
Whyles wee thochts o' leavin' wad steal owre my brain;
But, wi' courage, I dashed aye the tear frae my e'e,
When I thocht o' my shoon, an' my five shillin' fee.

An' Martinmas brocht me my lang-thocht-o' store,
An' proudly I coonted it twenty times o'er;
An' lang years hae fled, in a fortunate train,
But I never ance met wi' sic raptures again.
The sailor, juist safe through the wild breakers steer'd,
Proud Waterloo's victor, when Blucher appeared,
Ne'er felt what I felt, as I placed on the knee
O' a fond-hearted mither, my five shillin' fee.

THE PEDLAR AND HIS PACK.

WARM and sultry was the weather,
    Scarce the least cloud did appear,
Fermers had begun to gether
    In the produce o' the year.

Some were mawin', some were shearin',
    Busy wi' the yellow grain;
Some were cartin', some were clearin',
    Some securin' frae the rain.

Pedlar Rob, his rounds a-going—
    Thrang time wi' him a' the year,
Wind or rain, or hail or snowing,
    Still he was obliged to steer.

Took the road, and flung his wallet
    Owre his shou'der wi' a stick;
Cash! he couldna get a haul o't,
    Scanty was the ready "tick."

Scanty needfu's vex'd his noddle;
    Yet, what vex'd him ten times more,
Scarcely could he get a boddle
    For what goods he'd sold before.

Country wives were out a-gleanin',—
  Left nae siller, thochtless sluts!
Rob look'd queer, ye ken the meanin',
  What's a purse without the guts!

Mony a weary mile he trudget—
  Still nae siller—curse the fates!
Aye the heavier seem'd the budget,
  Can it be the same with States?

Aye the langer getting fainter,
  Almost doubling at the knee,
Feint a cottage could he enter,
  De'il a body could he see.

Drouthy was the weary packman,
  Wantin' drink but near nae toon;
Shou'der skinless, sair his back, man,
  Draps o' sweat fell on his shoon.

Trembling like a man in dotage,
  When the grave is drawing near,
Robin spied, at length, a cottage,
  Doon a green lane somewhat near.

Perhaps some miser's? little matter
  Tho' he's ane that starves a rat;
"Here," thought he, "I'll get some water,
  Sure they won't refuse me that."

Doon he went and gently knockit,
   Thocht to meet some feeling face ;
Vain his hope, the door was lockit—
   No' a mortal near the place.

Roun' he turn'd and curs'd the sheelin',
   Feelin' what nae tongue can tell :
Threw his wallet doon, and wheelin',
   Kick'd it madly as it fell.

" Down with you, and done for ever,
   Wi' this trudgin' trade I'm at !
Bruising heart, and lungs, and liver,
   Wi' a heavy lump like that !

" Can get nocht when stomach pinches,
   No' even water when I crave ;
Tearin' up a man by inches,
   Ready for an early grave.

" Man ! did I say ? mair like cuddy
   Through the villages I pass,
Wand'rin' like a beggar-body,
   Bearin' burdens like an ass.

" Hirplin', wi' an ugly wallet,
   Like a rogue frae place to place ;
Ped'lin' Packman ! as they ca' it,
   Ev'n the title brings disgrace.

"Ugly baggage! ye may lie there—
  Lie and rot there every clout,
Till some beggar, passing by thee,
  Tears yer cotton entrails out."

Scarcely had he stopp'd, when terror
  Changed the colour o' his cheek;
Weel it micht when, to his horror,
  Thus the pack began to speak:—

"Robin, I ha'e heard wi' patience
  A' yer vain and fuilish talk;
Noo pray hear twa observations
  Frae yer puir deserted pack.

"When we twa got first acquainted,
  What had you but worthless rhyme?
Were ye rich or mair contented
  Than you're at the present time?

"A' yer worth, and wealth, and riches,
  An' yer empty boast o' fame,
Wadna bocht a pair o' breeches,
  Wadna three times fill'd yer wame.

"A' your swearin' and pretencin'
  Caused me naething but a smile;
But, since that was your commencin',
  Hear me juist a little while."

"No! you goblin wallet bein',
  Tho' you're tongued like Balaam's ass,
When I hear ye doonricht leein',
  Hang me if I let it pass!

"Ere wi' you I was acquainted
  Then I lived quite free frae strife,
Ate and drank, and lived contented,
  Never wantin' a' my life.

"Life was then a round of pleasure,
  Every morning brocht its joys—
Work'd at will and, at my leisure,
  Ranted in my corduroys."

"Maybe never doonright wanted,
  Still o' mony a thing felt need;
Then it was ye howl'd and ranted
  In your corduroys indeed.

"Corduroys! and them sae clouted,
  Backside, foreside, knee'd an' a';
Even a body micht disputed
  What they were at first ava.

"Rinning juist at ilk' ane's biddin',
  Fear a birk yer back should scar,
Like a moudie in a midden,
  Howkin' 'mang the dirt and glaur.

"Noo ye'll talk o' froth and sweatin',
  Bearin' burdens like an ass;
Did I keep ye not in eatin',
  Troth you would be sweatin' less.

"Wha yer hungry wame's aye filling?
  What pits something in your pouch?
Wha provides you wi' a sheelin'
  Which no mortal man dare touch?

"Wha is't lets ye lie on feathers?
  Wha pits claes upon yer back?
Wha buys pens to write yer blethers?
  Wha the deevil! but yer pack?

"Mind ye'll ne'er get sic anither
  When in pairtin', me ye've "cut;"
Wha keeps frame and soul thegither?
  Is it me or is it not?

"If ye mean to try your luck then,
  Tak' me up ance mair and try;
If ye mean to end in kickin,'
  Kick again and let me lie.

"Either way, sir, I am willin';
  But resolve, noo, and be quick;
Either go and be a villain,
  Or come shou'der up your stick."

Rob, wha wasna void o' hearin',
   Listen'd to the Wallet's chat,
Heard its usefu' points up-clearin',
   And he felt the truth o' that.

Rob—high notions now misgiving,
   Ken'd, if he his brains could rack
Up as high's the mune, his living
   Still proceeded frae the pack—

Answered thus, " Why, a' that's in it,
   You and I ha'e lang been frien's,
Ne'er disputed till this minute,
   Tho' we've baith met mony scenes.

" But, what caus'd my wild oration,
   Mind and body baith got weak ;
Naething else but desperation
   Made me sae unmanly speak.

" But now come, dear pack, I hail you,
   I can bear thee without pain ;
Well enough I know thy value,
   We shall never fight again."

Rob resolved, and kept his fix'd way,
   With enthusiastic pluck,
All that afternoon, and next day,
   Meeting with the best o' luck.

Mortals, ye wha meet vexation,
  Never cowardly turn your back;
Changes come in every station,
  Mind the Pedlar and his Pack.

THE WIDOW'S AE COO.

AH, where's noo the cottage that stood by the moor,
Wi' its bricht bleezin' ingle an' bonny clean floor?
Its doun an' awa', no' a vestige appears,
Where in peace and content dwelt the widow for years.
She kept a wee coo, 'twas her leevin' an' pride,
She gethered her mouthfu' alang the roadside;
She was black owre the back, had a bonnie white broo,
An' a wee lassie herded the widow's ae coo.

Weel ken'd on the bye-road twa miles up and doon,
She lang held the favour o' ilka farm toon;
By master an' servant, by lad an' by lass,
It was "Harmless wee Hawkie, puir thing, let her pass."

The verra warst schuleboy wha gaed out the road,
Wha pelted ilk' cuddy an' spanghu'd ilk' toad,
In frien'ship an' feelin', ne'er passed but he threw
A handfu' o' grass to the widow's ae coo.

Wi' comforts contented the widow liv'd weel—
Her bing of potatoes, her kist fu' o' meal;
The least obligation she lo'ed to requite,
While the hameless an' wretched ne'er pass'd but
    her mite.
Wi' bonnie clean basket she gaed to the toon,
Wi' her sax pund a week amaist a' the year roun';
For milk an' for butter oor wide parish through
Couldna boast sic a beast as the widow's ae coo.

But a new race sprang up, an' their pride couldna
    bear
To see the wee coo by the road ony mair;
They threaten'd the widow wi' jail an' wi' law,
An' blamed her wee Hawkie wi' things she ne'er
    saw;
For foplin's wha daurna their daddies displease,
Made her aft an excuse for their blood's broken
    knees;
Even jolly auld gentlemen, trottin' hame fou',
Got their broken nose blam'd on the widow's ae coo.

Sae they forced her at length to put Hawkie away,
An' sair-hearted left her to wear out her day;
When owre frail to labour, an' owre blin' to sew,
A poor parish pauper they've made o' her noo.
An' where are we better though police gae by,
To pummel our beggars or pound our stray kye?
Could market nights speak, they would answer, I trew,
" Far waur, for there's ten tipsy accidents noo,
For ane in the days of the widow's ae coo."

SONG.

MY Love's a little country lass,
   Like me, unknown to fame,
Belonging to the rural class,
   I winna tell her name;
But she's endowed wi' every charm,
   The lassie I adore,
And happy dwells upon yon farm,
   Beside the banks of Orr.

I've seen now twenty winters' blast,
   And twenty springs so green,
My twentieth autumn's nearly past:
   My Love's in her eighteen;

Song.

Tho' young, she has a heart that's kind,
    A bosom that can feel;
She is the lass that's to my mind,
    The lassie I lo'e weel.

And oft I meet my bonnie lass;—
    But where I winna tell,
When, unperceived, she leaves the rest
    And meets me by hersel':
There's nought to me such pleasure yields—
    'Tis joys lent from above—
As walking through the dewy fields,
    At gloamin', wi' my love.

And tho' midst others I be dumb,
    And with you have no chat,
The time, dear lassie, yet will come
    I'll talk with you for that:
Then fare-ye-well, my bonnie lass,
    Thy name I'll not reveal
Until that time will come to pass
    We'll no' want to conceal.

SONG.

WHERE Galloway's hills
 And purling rills
Nature's face adorn;
 There can I trace
 My native place—
The spot where I was born.

 The glens and dales,
 The lochs and vales,
The hills that barren be;
 There's no' a place
 In Nature's face
More charming dear to me.

 Where winding Orr
 Flows to the shore,
Bedeck'd on every side
 With native flow'rs
 That sweetly pours
Their fragrant scents awide.

Song.

'Tis there, 'tis there
 The heart of Kerr
Loves best of places a',
 Tho' I must roam
 Far, far from home
To places far awa.

 There, native scenes
 And dearest frien's,
I leave them for a while,
 Yet full intent,
 When time is sent,
Again to see my Isle.

 Then fare-ye-well,
 My friends that dwell
Along the banks of Orr;
 Thy native Bard
 May yet be heard
Should he ne'er see you more.

MY FATHER'S ADDRESS TO HIS AULD DOG LADDIE.

AULD dog, it plain to me appears
    Ye're gaun the gate o' your forbears;
Ilk' member o' yer body wears
    Yer frame thegither,
And shows you're wearing doun wi' years
    To your auld mither.

I'm wae to think ye're gaun to leave me,
I never kenn'd ye to deceive me,
As true a dog—you will bereave me—
    As e'er was whalpit;
O! when I think on't, hoo it grieves me,
    Yet canna help it.

Time in a hurry rins awa,
To me it seems nae time ava
Since my auld dog, baith young and raw,
    A half-grown collie,
Ran yelpin' after cat and craw,
    Richt fu' o' folly.

But noo twal simmers hae gane past,
Twal winters, too, hae blawn their blast,
And three times four springs hae I cast
    In terra's bowels
My pickle seed (that's nae sae vast)—
    Hoo fast time rolls!

You've been a famous dog, and art
As true as ever at the heart;
But auld age makes yer body smart,
    Sae fu' o' pain,
An' winna let ye do yer part
    As ye wad fain.

When young nane wi' ye could compare
To rin a race or scent a hare,
Or tent the kye wi' muckle care,
    Auld thriftfu' tykie;
Folks a' kenn'd ye belang'd to Kerr,
    'Cause nane was like ye.

Wi' coat o' grey an' lugs o' broun,
A ringlet white yer neck went roun',
A streak o' white gaed owre yer croun;
    Yer tail sae free
Hung curl'd owre yer back aboon,
    Nane were like thee.

Address to a Dog.

That simmer my wee Tam was born,
I mind it weel, ae sunny morn,
When wading through the dewy corn
  To catch the mare,
As passin' by the Pairtrick Thorn
  Up starts a hare.

I never bade ye then to rin,
But ye were no' to haud or bin',
For, tho' I tried to keep ye in,
  Aff, aff ye hurried—
My fegs, ye nimbly tried her win',
  Sune she was worried.

That was a sma' thing o' itsel',
Yet future prospects it did tell,
For aye frae that time could I spell,
  An' plainly see,
If ye but lieved till ye were aul',
  What ye would be.

The herd boy aften times wi' thee,
When herding owre ayont the lea,
In cauld days when the busy bee
  Kept in its cell,
And birds o' passage cross'd the sea,
  Mair warm to dwell.

There aften-times wi' thee, auld dog,
He would traverse baith hill an' bog,
Running wi' thee—outlawing rogue—
  He thocht nae ill o't,
When some lam'd hare had ta'en the scrog,
  To gang an' kill it.

When snaw was cov'rin' a' the grun,
Hoo aft, weel pleas'd wi' dog an' gun,
I've rang'd the fiel's, when Tam, my son,
  A toddlin' wee thing,
Was keen as I to see the fun,
  Tho' we got naething.

Redcastle hills on every side
Wi' yelp ye've made to echo wide,
Wi' mony a spang an' mony a stride
  Thou hast gaen owre them,
Stickin' yer tusks fast in the hide
  O' hares galorem.

For wi' puir puss ye were'na sparin',
Ye mony o' them gi'ed their fairin';
There's no a field in a' the Baron',
  I'll safely say,
But ye ha'e nimbly catch'd a hare in,
  Or aiblins twae.

Address to a Dog.

Yer bonny tail ye wad hae stretched
While rigs at every spang ye fetched,
And your keen eye so fiercely watched
    Puss rin before;
Short was the race till she was catched
    An' tumbled o'er.

At nicht thou wert a famous guard
To barn, to peat-house, an' to yard—
To them ye paid as much regard
    As if ye ken't aye
Auld winter wi' his hoary beard
    Wad need o' plenty.

When strange cats cam' about the hoose,
Wi' them ye played the verra deuce—
Aft hae I kenn'd ye tak' puir puss
    Fast in yer gums,
And make her back crack like a louse
    Atween twa thumbs.

The fumarts a' times shunn'd yer face,
And at a distance kept, and wise;
Wi' vermin thou wert never nice
    O' what degrees;—
An' worried weasels, rats, and mice,
    By twa's and three's.

But noo ye're wearin' near yer en',
Ye're like mankin' at three-score-ten—
Short i' the wun, ye stoop an' ben',
    Till juist a wee
Shall put a finish to yer pain,
    Nae mair to be.

Ah, time! ah, time! what hast thou torn?
What hast thou in the warl' not worn?
A' mortal things ye treat wi' scorn,
    Baith great and sma;
An' sune the dounwards path are borne,
    Men, dogs, an' a'.

Yer hearin' noo is seen to fail,
Yer e'en, ance bricht, look dim an' pale,
An' something, since you lost yer tail
    Amang the fause anes,
Tells me ye're scarcely like yersel',
    Or what ye was ance.

   . . . .

Ah! my auld dog, ye little ken
Thae mortals we ca' sons o' men,
Wha' treat your maister wi' disdain
    An' empty slur,
An' tell him openly an' plain
    To shoot his cur.

Address to a Dog.

They say auld age will make ye bad,
An' then nae doubt ye will gae mad—
I should be vex'd and unco sad
    If sic I saw;
But ye shall never dee, auld lad,
    By " Jeddart law."

They're but a set o' numskull bodies,
Possess'd wi' nae mair sense than cuddies;
I'll sooner see them a' in wuddies,
    An' twisted fast,
Ere I shall make my puir auld Laddie
    Sae draw his last!

Yes, sooner see the barn in fire,
Or shoot the best coo in the byre,
Ere I shall throw ye in a mire,
    To meet yer death;
Or hang ye wi' a cord or wire,
    To stop yer breath.

But let them a' say what they like,
Ye'se dee a fair death yet, auld tyke—
No' at the backside o' a dyke,
    Like ony blackguard!
But ye shall dee, for a' their fyke,
    In barn or stackyard.

Address to a Dog.

They'll ca' me noo a fool, nae doubt,
For rousin' sae' a wee dumb brute—
Wi' ony o' them I'll dispute,
    An' prove it too?
There's some, wha wear nae paw nor cloot,
    Micht learn frae you.

Oh! if mankind would but agree,
And live in social unity,
As true as ye ha'e been to me
    In your career!
This world to saunts micht ever be
    Maist truly dear.

Then should I live till I be grey,
And throw the warld's cares away;
And wi' grand-children sport an' play
    Upon the green—
The spot where laddie's put away
    Shall still be seen.

Then will I tell each little one
How oft times wi' thee I've had fun—
How often thou hast races run
    O'er ditches clinkin',
Wi' ilka feat thou's ever done
    That I can think on.

Sae gang yer ways, an' streak yer back
Aneath a corn or clover stack,
To keep ye snug I'se no' be slack,
    And, tho' I'm poor,
For ocht that's guid ye winna lack
    To my last hoor.

SONG.

WHEN the setting sun cast a long shade from the west,
  On yon hill where together the larch and fir grows,
On a green turf at gloaming I sat down to rest,
  And, musing on Nature, I sank to repose.

Chorus.
    I had thought on the maid of yon village when wake,
    And slumbering still on my fancy she dwelt.

Song.

For now in my dreams my fair charmer appear'd,
   And more lovely than ever she seemèd to be,
In a neat rural cot, where each other we cheer'd,
   And I thought none on earth were so happy as we.
     Chorus.—I had thought, &c.

And fondly I claspèd my love in my arms,
   And as fond on my bosom she seem'd to recline;
And happy I felt when I prais'd all her charms,
   But happier far when I thought she was mine.
     Chorus.—I had thought, &c.

But the wind whistling over my green grassy bed,
   Aroused me as Phœbus shot out his last beam;
In a moment of time I had lost my fair maid,
   I awoke from my rest, and—'twas only a dream.

     Chorus.

   I had thought on the maid of yon village when wake,
    And slumbering still on my fancy she dwelt.

SONG.—THE LASS THAT LIVES BESIDE THE MILL.

'TWAS summer when the woods were green,
   And all in Nature's face seem'd fair,
One morn when hares were sporting seen,
   And larks sang sweetly in the air;
Admiring Nature's wond'rous law,
   When musing by the wooded hill,
With raptur'd gaze 'twas first I saw
   The lass that lives beside the mill.

The flow'rs ope'd forth with various dye,
   The birds sang sweet their mates to call;
All Nature's beauties seemed to vie,
   With her whose charms outstripp'd them all.
Her lovely form and beauteous face
   Show'd Nature's power to mould with skill;
Adorn'd was she with every grace—
   The lass that lives beside the mill.

As on she pass'd my heart was rais'd,
   With quicker pace my pulse did beat,
As thus on Nature's work I gaz'd,
   Her last, her best, her most complete.

The Lass beside the Mill.

Her looks so coy I'll ne'er forget,
   My heart enrapt was caught at will;
With fancy's eye I picture yet—
   The lass that lives beside the mill.

Tho' with the maid not yet acquaint,
   I well could see the heart refin'd;
Her lovely eye too well did paint
   An innocent and artless mind.
As happy as the lamb that plays
   Amongst the heather on the hill,
So happy could I spend my days
   With her that lives beside the mill.

Then free from every care and strife,
   When all my wants were turned my own;
How happy then to spend my life,
   With her to rise, with her lie down.
And when old age runs out life's tide,
   And we our season did fulfil,
Then I'd resign, and sleep beside
   The lass that lives beside the mill.

CUPID'S CONQUEST.

"WHY tarried ye so long, my son—
    Where have you been so late?
What! softening down some maiden's heart
    Whose beau wants her estate?
Or shooting at some youth to woo
    Some maiden young and coy?
Or had you extra work to do?"
    Cried Venus to her boy—

"I had no extra work to do
    To-day, I freely grant;
I vex'd no young expecting things
    By shooting their rich aunt;
Nor bent I bow at blushing maid,
    So full of hopes and fears;
I went to see a bachelor wed
    Who'd baffl'd me for years."

"You showed him youth and beauty, then,
    With wit and sense refined?
You pointed out some lady fair,
    With noble traits of mind?
Or, selfishly, you showed him land,
    And whole streets in a row?
For few old bachelors can withstand
    Such tempting things below."

" O yes, I showed him wit and worth
    For many a day gone by;
I showed him youth and beauty, but
    He turned away his eye :
When years increased, the golden bait
    I held out to this man ;
But he had been a bachelor yet
    Had I not changed my plan.

" I led him to a little maid,
    Not forwardsome nor shy;
She helped his dripping great-coat off,
    And hung it up to dry :
She bade him sit, and brought a chair,
    And spoke so kindly, too :
I hit him ere he was aware,
    And ne'er had less to do.

" *Let wit, and wealth, and beauty plead,*
    Their conquests are not small;
The kind word and obliging deed
    Can conquer more than all:
Can conquer so, that this I'll say—
    If maidens should pursue
That simple plan, in short time they
    Would leave me nought to do."

JOHN FROST.

THERE cam' an auld carle doon frae the north,
    Awa frae the polar sea,
'Twas a pity he ever got over the Forth,
    For a cruel auld carle was he.
'Twas the wee dull day when he reach'd oor place,
    A stranger alone—we felt for his case,
Wi' his auld grey heid and his dignified face,
    An' as calm as calm could be.

He painted trees on the window panes,
    His colours were licht and blue,
He seemed an auld carle wi' fertile brains,
    And a very fine pencil, too.
Some ither wee tricks he played at nicht,
But naething at first to cause ony fricht,
And aye as the sun appeared in sicht
    He melted awa like dew.

But at length he turn'd quite bauld and rude,
    He cared for the sun nae mair;
He brocht the wild beasts oot o' the wood,
    And the wee birds frae the air.

He clasp'd the loch in an icy urn,
He chain'd the pleuch, he seal'd up the burn,
He wadna let a water wheel turn,
   And stripped the fields quite bare.

He slidder'd the pavements a' aboot,
   To break folks' legs an' arms,
He rudely turn'd the gardeners oot,
   And ruined puir Flora's charms.
Frae beauty's cheek he stole the rose,
He chill'd her heels, and he pinch'd her toes,
And he daub'd his blue brush owre her nose,
   And filled her wi' alarms.

He travell'd the country round and round,
   No spot untouched left he;
He chased the moles deep into the ground,
   And the wild fowl to the sea.
He search'd our cottages through and through,
Cam' in at the door and gaed oot at the flue,
His bitter breath turn'd sae bad it slew
   The cushie doo in the tree.

He made the fireless cottager mourn,
   The bare-leggèd beggar greet,
The wearied traveller ne'er to return,
   But stiffened him on his seat.

Wi' fangs mair fierce than the merciless shark,
He followed the course of the storm-toss'd bark,
And grappled wi' mariners in the dark,
   And bit off their hands and feet.

'Twas strange what he did in his savage mood,
   And far ayont human ken,
Yet still mair strange sic a monster should
   Hae been worshippèd by men.
Yet frae dawn to dusk would his votaries stan',
Wi' tramps on their feet and besoms in han',
While the curling stane an' the skips comman'
   Rang loud through each lowlan' glen.

But there cam' a brave warrior oot o' the south,
   An' his name was General Thaw,
Warm and kind were the words o' his mouth
   When oor pitious case he saw.
Bauldly advancing, he challeng'd auld John,
Wha grinn'd wi' contempt and bade him begone;
So they mustered their troops, and the battle cam'
   on,
   It was wha should gie rule an' law.

Frost focht like a man in the maddest despair,
   And Thaw like a man for his richt,
And they struggl'd in earth and they struggl'd in
   air,
   Like giants of vigour and micht.

And days, and lang dreary nichts went round,
As they combated every inch of ground,
Till doon cam' auld Frost wi' a desperate wound,
   And he fled like a ghost frae licht.

Noo the pleughman is turning the clod o'er again,
   And prood is the gull and the craw;
The daisy's beginning to peep on the plain,
   An' the burns are run off wi' the snaw.
The pairtrick at e'en is mair sweet in his cry,
The lav'rocks are tuning their notes in the sky,
An' a thousan' young flow'rs will be here by-and-by:
   Our thanks to auld General Thaw.

AN AUTUMN EVE:
AN EPISTLE TO MY BROTHER JAMES.

WHEN Autumn's robes had crown'd the field,
   And reapers did the sickle wield,
One evening—when the band to yield
     Had thought it best,
As coming night their toils concealed,
     And gave them rest.

An Autumn Eve.

In loving pairs they homeward hie,
The reaping hooks are all laid by;
Now round the supper board they ply,
  And eager sup,
Whilst rural social mirth and joy
  Kept spirits up.—

I put my sickle in the thatch,
Of supper took a hasty snatch,
Then, silent lifting up the latch,
  I left the fun,
To climb yon hill and, silent, watch
  The setting sun.

The day drew quickly to a close,
And all in nature sought repose;
No music on the ear arose
  From warbling throats,
Save where the Robin midst the boughs
  Tun'd his last notes.

With never-ceasing rushing din
I heard the falling distant linn,
In Spottes glen, ere its streams begin
  To join the Orr,
Rising and falling as the win'
  Blew it before.

An Autumn Eve.

Whim-pleas'd, I wandered on my way,
And view'd the fast-expiring day
Give place to sober twilight gray,
  Whilst eastern skies
Foretold the moon, in pale array,
  Would soon arise.

The owl—that screeching bird of night—
Already had begun its flight;
I view'd the stars which, now in sight,
  Grew thicker still,
Until I'd reach'd the farthest height
  Of Holie's hill.

Surrounded there by verdant wood,
I on the vacant summit stood,
Where barren soil and tempests rude
  Leave bare the crown,
Then, wrapt in silent musing mood,
  I sat me down.

I mused on younger years, when we
Of every anxious care were free,
The bright school days, ere you and me
  Thought of the strife
That met us, launch'd upon the sea
  Of busy life.

On other days I turned my mind,
When we for some pursuit inclin'd,
Though many a rock and adverse wind
    Lay in our bay;
Still, judging we some shoal should find,
    Hope led the way.

I mused some time on scenes now past,
And, running o'er my lifetime fast,
I came to where we parted last—
    Ev'n that same nook,
Where, with dimm'd eye, I backward cast
    The last sad look.

Whilst musing deep on themes like these,
A trem'lous noise came with the breeze,
Then rustling through amongst the trees
    Which round me grew,
Two maidens fair, in grace and ease,
    Appear'd in view.

I felt that something inward rise
That comes when taken by surprise,
Yet, still composed my wond'ring eyes,
    And with fixed stare
I longing strove to recognise
    Such features fair.

I gaz'd, as I would gaze them through,
But, O, such forms I never knew;
Then I bethought me if 'tis true
    There was a Nine;
Such features as appear'd in view,
    Must be Divine.

In years they seemed near to mysel'—
One score, perhaps, but that was all;
Proportioned fair, not over tall,
    They seemed to be;
And figures such as pleasèd well
    A lover's e'e.

Advancing to me with a smile,
I viewed their garments all, the while—
No airy, flippant, gaudy style,
    But gowns and plaids;
The costume of our native isle
    Adorned the maids.

Soon on the rocky height they land,
Where for their coming I did stand,
With calf-skin cap fast in my hand,
    As manners bade us—
And thus I spoke, "I'm at command,
    Your servant, ladies!"

The nearest then, with beaming eye
And rosy cheek, thus made reply—
" You who now view'st the azure sky,
    Where stars shine clear ;
Shall know, with wonder, by-and-by
    What brings us here !

" Two Gallovidian sisters we—
By name, I'm known as Poetry ;
Genius of Agriculture, she,
    My sister there ;
This night we come to visit thee
    In open air."

" Far fam'd exalted maids," said I,
" Dost thou descend from realms on high
To visit me, a rustic boy
    Without a name ;
Unlike to those who soar and fly—
    On wings of fame."

" 'Tis so, young man, thou art, most sure,
Unheeded, friendless, and obscure,
And what the world may call as poor—
    But there 'tis o'er ;
For with those pains you here endure
    There's better store.

"And you must also ere this know,
What ills attend man's life below;
Oftimes an endless source of woe
    His lifetime fills;
And where the greater riches flow,
    Are most of ills.

"'Tis that makes man grow wearied here,
And look up to another sphere;
If everything on earth were dear
    To human hearts,
Mankind would never wish to steer
    To other parts.

"'Tis not with rich, 'tis not with great,
'Tis not with leaders of a State,
'Tis not with those whose lucky fate
    In power excels,
That happiness has greatest weight,
    Or chiefly dwells.

"The homely, untaught, rustic hind,
With plain uncultivated mind,
Quite ignorant of what's refin'd,
    Or deep read lore;
Is not one whit his lord behind
    In blissful store.

"Two favourites of thy chief delight,
We from a distance took our flight,
To visit thee this Autumn night,
  On this lone spot;
To let thee know (though not in sight)
  What friends thou'st got.

"Our favourite thou hast been for long,
For when thou at the plough wert throng,
We saw thee weave thy rustic song,
  In early years;
And knew thy wish to shine among
  Thy low compeers.

"Continue still," addressed the maid,
"Thy plough and poetry," she said,
"Condemning vice, be not afraid—
  Make virtue shine;
And thou shalt ever have our aid—
  Both hers and mine."

This said, she fell back in the rear,
And whispered in her sister's ear—
Then in a voice distinct and clear,
  By far the best;
The Genius of the Plough drew near,
  And thus addrest:—

"My much respected, favourite lad,
Unto these words I cannot add;
But, oh! you better never had
  Have heard what's said;
If by neglect you be so mad,
  As lose our aid.

"In younger years I did bewail
To see thee leave thy native vale;
I saw thee take a sad farewell
  Of all our plains,
With some foreign genii to prevail,
  For sake of gains.

"With joy I saw thee, native swain,
Return home to thy land again;
I proudly saw thee till the plain
  When Spring had sway;
And viewed thee cut the yellow grain
  This Autumn day.

"Continue still to weave thy lay
When at the plough from day to day;
Till o'er these fields where now you stray,
  And oft hast felt,
The plough-boys yet unborn may say
  'Here Kerr once dwelt.'

"But if again Fate should decree
You leave your native spot and me,
In foreign lands to follow thee
    Is past my power;
But Poetry with thee shall flee,
    Where'er you tour.

"As parting word—in whate'er land
You chance to roam, make this your plan—
Let nought that will ashame the man
    Your theme divide;
But grow aye closer, if you can,
    To Virtue's side."

Then from their plaids forthwith they drew
Two instruments of music new,
In shape of harps of golden hue,
    But brighter far;
Reflecting—shining—upwards threw
    Each twinkling star.

Then, in the deep'ning twilight gray,
They leaning down began to play;
And striking some melodious lay,
    Which had no bounds,
Enchanted, I fast swooned away
    Mid heavenly sounds.

How long I lay to me's unknown,
But when I woke the maids were gone;
Above, each twinkling star clear shone,
    And round the hill
I nothing saw, or voice heard none—
    But all was still.

The moon was far above *Lang Fell*,
The wild ducks quacked in mossy vale;
The thick'ning mist o'ercame the dale—
    No more I stay'd;
But bidding earth a short farewell,
    Slipp'd home to bed.

NANNY BELL.

ON the outskirts of a village,
    In a cottage by itsel',
A retired spot for auld age,
    There liv'd honest Nanny Bell.

Lang wi' cares had Nanny striven,
    Oft' had fortune turn'd her tail,
Oft' to her last shift been driven,
    Noo at last got unco frail.

Ae day sitting by the fire,
  Owre her vexing cares she ran,
Thinking there was nae ane nigh her,
  To hersel' she thus began :—

" Surely there's nane in the nation,
  Frae the farthest east to wast,
Leeves in sic a situation
  As I leeve mysel' at last.

" A' my best resources fail me,
  Never can I pay the rent,
They can only tak' and jail me,
  I maun only tak' what's sent.

" My best claes are in the broker's,
  Wi' my puir man's coat and vests,
A' my hens are turn'd to clockers,
  A' my deuks ta'en hidden nests.

" My wee yowie's crowl'd and crabbèd,
  Her twa lambs droon'd in a ditch,
And my pig tak's fits, and's scabbèd,
  I'm the prey of some auld witch.

" My wee yaird is like a desert,
  Ingans, leeks, and carrots fail;
And that cock—I'll stick his gizzard—
  Scrapes the cabbage and the kail.

"Everything that I hae gotten—
　Claes and furniture, my whole,
Sune, alas, will a' be rotten
　In this reekit, rainy hole.

"Everything is gaun to ruin,
　Nocht this season can me save;
O, that I ne'er saw a new ane!
　O, that I was in my grave!"

As she thus was sad lamenting,
　Something at her door play'd pat;
Baith her grief and anger venting,
　Nanny cried, "What limmer's that?"

"Wha's wee rascal's that keeps knockin',
　O' your impudence no slack?
Stop till I lay by my stockin',
　Faith I'll break your ugly back!"

Still it knock'd, till Nanny bounded
　Wi' a fury owre the floor;
Back she cam', as much confounded,
　'Twas ane gentle at the door.

"Hoo d'ye do, sir, pray walk in, sir,"
　(Nanny scarce ken'd what to say);
"If for dubble ye can win, sir,"—
　He did Nanny soon obey.

Doun he sat, and wi' her crackit
  On the fineness of the day;
After he had some time talkit,
  Thus to Nanny he did say:—

"'Tis not my intent to draw ye
  Into ony lengthened tale;
Tell me truly if they ca' ye,
  Name and surname, Nanny Bell."

"Yes," said she, "that's what they ca'd me,
  And that's what they ca' me yet,
'Cept when ill-tongued loons hae scal'd me,
  Ne'er anither did I get!"

"That's a' richt, then, what relations
  Ha'e ye gotten, Nanny tell?"
"I ha'e some in different stations,
  Some poor bodies like mysel'.

"Some wha've got a little higher,
  But wha think me no sae guid;
Ca' them frien's! they ca' me liar,
  Sweir I'm no' ae drap o' bluid.

"Rich and puir, them a' thegither,
  Little thocht to me hae cost,—
To an only, dearest brither,
  Whom I mony years hae lost.

Nanny Bell.

" 'Tis noo thretty years and better
   Since our Johnnie gaed abroad,
But for lang I've got nae letter,
   He's langsyne gane to his God."

" You're the very one, 'tis granted,
   Yes, as sure's that kitten mews;
You're the very wife I wanted,
   I'm sent here to tell you news.

" News will set you yet carousing,
   News that will your old heart cheer,—
You've fa'en heir to twenty thousand,
   Near one thousand pounds a year!"

" You should ne'er make sport o' auld age,"
   Nanny to him did reply;
" Ere ye lie beneath earth's foliage
   You may be as poor as I!"

" Nanny, my words true you'll find them,
   Johnny's deid, and gane awa;
A big fortune left behind him—
   You're the heiress to it a'.

" See, there is his ain handwriting!"
   Nanny got her specs to see't,
Saw it was his ain inditing,
   Could do naething else but greet.

Soon she got what John did leave her,
   For the tale it was quite true ;
And, no person to bereave her
   Of what rightly was her due,

Long she lived, in peace and plenty,
   And seem'd grateful aye to be ;
And this will, as a momento,
   Made when she was gaun to dee :—

" After paying all my due debts,
   Which are sma', and very few ;
And expense of undertakers,
   Which my pocket cash will do,

" Everything as I possess'd it,
   Shall be sold, or gi'en away ;
And the capital invested
   Where it shall for ever stay,—

" To remain and be a sure rock,
   In the name of Nanny Bell ;
And the int'rest gi'en to poor folk,
   Like what she was ance hersel'."

SONG.

LASSIE wi' the tartan plaidie,
   Rosy cheek an' beaming eye,
Wil't thou wed a ploughman laddie?
   Say, my dear, you will comply.

Unto thee I will be true, lass,
   On my breast thou shalt recline;
None on earth I'll have but you, lass,
   Say, my dear, then, you'll be mine.

By day I'll toil, an' when weary,
   To my home I'll haste away;
Then at night I'll clasp my dearie
   Till the dawning of the day.

Say thou'rt willing to wed me, lass,
   We'll get joined in Hymen's bands,
If you're willing, I am free, lass,
   With thee, dearie, to join hands.

Thou shalt ever find thy lover
   What he promises to be;
Rolling years shall but discover
   How much, lassie, I love thee.

ADDRESS TO A CORN.

THOU wee mischief man ca's corn,
    Wi' thy tormenting head of horn,
Ten thousand times waur than a thorn,
        Or ony prick,
Lang has my little toe thee borne,
        An' to't ye'll stick.

Wi' sharpened knife I've thocht nae crime
To cut and pare thee mony a time;
I've got apothecary's brine,
        And paid for't dear.
Yet, spite of a' their saut and lime,
        Thou still art here.

I've heard folks say what's in the bane
Out of the flesh will ne'er be gane;
It's my opinion thou alane
        First form'd the tale,
For wi' yer gnawing pain there's nane
        Proves't half so well.

Address to a Corn.

Fast fixed and far spread is thy root,
Whilst from the bane thy branches shoot,
And on the surface do look oot,
    In proud disdain,
Tormenting my poor aching foot
    With dreadful pain.

Ev'n now I feel your cursèd sting,
Aye, there it plays ding-ding, ding-ding;
Ye villain, could I only bring
    Ye frae your den,
What tae ye next should enter in
    I'd let ye ken.

Tho' sma' in size you're great in micht,
And torturing's your chief delicht,
Tormenting me baith day and nicht
    Wi' pain eternal;
The very thocht's eneugh to fricht
    A fiend infernal.

Or when upon the beaten road
My foot against a stane plays daud,
With beating heart it puts me mad,
    Whilst I, poor Rob,
Roar oot, and maun do, if I had
    Patience like Job.

Address to a Corn.

And then to see me jump and start
If hit upon the tender part,
O, hoo it strikes me to the heart,
  And birrs the strings
As when from bow, an arrow darts
  On flying wings.

A burning gum, frae gnawing tooth,
Is to auld age, or sprightly youth,
A bad companion in the mouth—
  A horrid pain,
But when compared with thee, forsooth,
  What is it then?

With aching tooth you've but to yawn,
When with the pinchers it is drawn,
But thou tormenting devil's spawn,
  Thou cursèd corn!
Cut thee—we end where we began
  By next day morn.

O, where's thy match in a' the nation,
In powers of growth and generation,
For, cut thee out of observation,
  In twa-three hours
Again you will hae ta'en your station
  Wi' stronger powers.

Address to a Corn.

I've borne you now a lang, lang while,
I've walk'd with you a thousand mile,
I've clambered over mony a stile,
  Limping wi' thee,
Yet still from May until April
  Ye stick to me.

Wi' you there's never thocht o' rueing
As in a vice my toe ye're screwing,
And wi' yer talons deep are strewing
  The venom o'er,
So that I'm like to want a new one,
  By thy curs'd power.

But if to me ye hae been sent
To tease, to torture, and torment,
So that in time I may repent
  By feeling pain,
I'm unco fear'd your good intent
  Will be but vain.

But may each one of Britain's foes,
And every mother's son of those
Who British liberties oppose,
  And don't preserve them,
Have twenty corns upon their toes—
  They well deserve them!

THE PLOUGH'S ADDRESS TO ROBERT M'KINNELL.

"WHA is't, this cauld November morn,
    That grasps me firmly by the horn?
Ha'e a' my frien's left me forlorn
    To strange embraces?
I ne'er was fond, sin' I was born,
    O' unken'd faces.

"But frown at fate it's what I dinna,
And blame you, sir, it's what I winna,
But surely in my life I've seen a
    Face like thine:
Come, tell me, is your sirname Kinna?"
    Quo' Rab, "That's mine."

"I ken your pedigree," quo' Katie,
"And haena muckle cause to hate ye,
Tho' mony a plooing chiel may beat ye,
    In twa-three year,
As sure's your dad leeves in Da'beattie,
    Some will look queer.

The Plough's Address.

" My maister was a rhyming chiel,
Trouth whyles he wish'd me at the de'il,
For when he couldna plough it weel,
  He took and blam'd me,
Gaun like a pend'lum through a fiel',
  He quite asham'd me.

" But, Rab, ye winna be like him,
But keep yer airns in proper trim,
And we will never try to slim
  Red-land or lea,
But make oor wark baith neat and trim,
  To please the e'e.

" Noo, Rabbin, lad, just keep your eye
Between the pownies and the sky,
And never talk wi' stan'ers by
  Or ony cronie,
And we will make the furrows lie
  Baith straight and bonnie."

SONG.

Air—"Buy a Broom."

I'M a young country lassie, both robust and healthy,
   I'm born to no fortune, whatever be sent,
Yet, though I am poor, what care I for the wealthy,
   When I move in that sphere which is blest with content?

What care I for great folks, or yet for their scorning,
   My fate or my fortune I never deplore:
Contented, I rise with the lark every morning,
   I'm a young country lassie—my dad lives in Orr.

I'm acquainted with those both in high and low stations,
   And even with those who to fortune lay claim;
Yet what do I care for all friends or relations—
   There's a lad I like best, but I'll no' tell his name.

Song.

His look and his language my bosom bewitches,
   And I am the lassie he seeks to adore;
Then what do I care for this wide world's riches,
   I'm a young country lassie—my dad lives in Orr.

Tho' with contempt I'm looked at by wealthier maidens,
   Who in silks and in laces dress up like a queen;
Yet when I am clothed in my own country plaidin',
   As happy as them I can dance o'er the green.

Then while I remain still a stranger to sorrow,—
   Whilst health, peace, and content, I still have in store;
As long's without dread, I can rest for the morrow,
   I'll never forsake the sweet banks of the Orr.

WRITTEN IN ROBERT M'KINNELL'S PIPE-MUSIC BOOK,

9TH NOVEMBER, 1842.

HAIL to the pipes! to Scotland dear,
    Which oftimes roused her patriot band:
What Scottish soul but loves to hear
    The music of his native land.

But never may *thy* rustic reed,
    M'Kinnell, sound in lands afar,
To march o'er fields, where vultures feed,
    Or mingle in the din of war.

May peace and plenty with thee dwell,
    To tune thy pipes, or till the plain;
And long may Scotia's hill and dell
    Re-echo back thy peaceful strain.

LINES

On hearing that some of the Members of Dumfries Presbytery were angry any one should oppose the introduction of Mr Fyfe to St. Mary's Church, Dumfries.

WHEN Kings said organs should praise God,
   It raised our father's bristles;
Their very heart's blood dyed the sod
   To keep out "Kists o' Whistles."
But, oh! how changed from what she was—
   Our Kirk there's so much strife in't,
Her very clergy's mad because
   They cannot place a *fife* in't.

VERSES ON THE DEATH OF A YOUNG LADY'S LAP-DOG, NAMED TERRY.

ALAS! poor little Terry's dead,
   His earthly course is o'er;
Alas! poor little Terry's fled,
   To tarry here no more.

On the Death of a Lap-Dog.

No more he at the door will stay,
    When waiting my command;
No more around his mistress play,
    Or lick his master's hand.

When in the East the bright sun-rise
    Shall usher in new day,
And Nature's fair and cloudless skies
    Shall tempt my feet to stray,

No more will Terry run before,
    All dangers to expel;
No more the winding path explore,
    Or yet come back to tell.

Nor on his master, Bryce, await,
    To walk when day grows cool,
Or meet him joyful at the gate
    When he comes home from school.

When to the village I repair,
    No little dog so true
My reticule will carry there,
    As Terry used to do.

But why his qualities recite?
    I'll silent o'er them pass;
'Twould take a day, from morn to night,
    To tell what use he was.

On the Death of a Lap-Dog.

A good companion, in his place,
    A faithful servant too;
Time from my memory won't efface
    The little dog so true.

TERRY'S EPITAPH.

Here Terry lies, no more to rise,
    No more my basket carry,
No more to ope his death-shut eye,
    Alas! poor little Terry.

Laugh not at epitaphs on dogs!
    His name, why not preserve it?
The same is often done to rogues,
    Who don't so well deserve it.

SONG.

UR old neighbour Tom got his bottle well
    primed,
  And thus to his good wife did say:
"With our friends, don't you think, 'twould be very
    well timed,
  Should we broach it on *auld* New Year's Day?"

Tom's dame, who was never behind him through
    life,
  Whenever to counsel they went,
Declared with a smile, like a good sterling wife,
  That with pleasure she'd back his intent.

"The doctor," says Tom, " who attends to our nags,
  We must have at our spread, if in trim;
With the old skipper Laird, from Colvend's rugged
    crags,
  For we can't do at all without him!

"And Redcastle Rob will be keen of the job,
  For there's none on earth fonder of fun!
These three I'll have o'er, as old cronies of yore,"—
  And his wife said his will should be done.

Tom's friends were invited, and soon they were
    there,
  In spite of foul weather and fog;
Whilst the dame spread a feast that might serve a
    Lord May'r,
  Just by way of a preface for grog.

Soon the table was clear'd, and Tom's bottle
    appear'd.
  "Now," says Tom, "I want fair up and down!
So here's to Queen Vic., may her foes go to Nick,
  And our Thistle still stick to its crown."

"Prime, and load again quick," cried old Tom, like
    a chief,
  "Make ready! present, lads, and fire!
May the New Year attend to the needy's relief,
  And send us more corn than his sire."

Our bumpers we mix'd to our noble sel's next:
  "May we long live in peace with the laws!
May our wives aye look sweet, and our ends easy
    meet!"
  So we drank it with rounds of applause.

"Come now," cried the skipper, "let's rest on our
    oars,"
  When the doctor, beginning to sing!
Went an octave or more higher up than before,
  Till he made the old building to ring.

"Now," said Tom, "fill a glass to the doctor's success,
  May disorders fly off at his bid,
May his bolus and pills cure the double he kills,
  And no trouble e'er bother his head!"

There, with tale and with song full of pith, but not long,
  The hours danced away rank and file;
Like the train of George Fox, we avowed not to box,
  But we spoke by the spirit in style.

For our skipper shipped every full tumbler did pass,
  Our ploughman, with fun on his phiz,
Clean lifted the hinting of every fresh glass,
  Whilst the doctor anatomised his.

At length there came in a disturber of peace,
  Not a moment the creature would sit:
Said his name was Old Time, and his tongue would not cease,
  As he gave us broad hints to be quit.

With a loud extra knock every hour on the clock,
  He warned us no longer to stay;
But we each filled our "gun" with the best Glasgow spun,
  Just to smoke our disturber away.

"Come, my friends," said old Tom, "take another
    glass in,
  'Tis the very best thing you can do;
'Tis the only receipt that can smother his din!"
  So we tasted, and found it was true.

But he knockèd still more than he had done before,
  And seemed as he'd pester our lives,
So we rose every one, having finished our can,
  And journied home pleased to our wives.

LINES

ON A BROTHER RHYMER WHO, WITH SOME OF HIS
NEIGHBOURS, SOLD THEIR WATER PUMP, AND
DRANK THE PRICE O'T.

'TWAS He alone, who knows the heart,
    To prove Himself divine,
Did once in Canaan's land convert
    The water into wine.
But Poet G***, even Christians own,
    Once played a trick as handy,—
He took his water pump alone
    And turned it into brandy?

THE POET'S EPITAPH.

HERE lies a bard who could not Fame's steep clim'—
Not quite earth-tired, but *that* was tired of him;
Ah! he had many a folly, many a whim,
And even now is just in the same trim
As when he used to move each living limb:
You can't guess how? but I'll explain in full—
For even now there's *maggots in his skull.*

www.ingramcontent.com/pod-product-compliance
Lightning Source LLC
Chambersburg PA
CBHW031348160426
43196CB00007B/781